Praise for *Problem Solved*

"In my 25 years reporting on social innovation, I've found that what distinguishes the most successful organizations is how they minimize risk, pursue opportunity, track results, and plan ahead. The AREA Method described in *Problem Solved* offers an accessible and systematic approach for anyone to do this: It shows how to break down complex decisions into manageable steps, and provides a disciplined method to identify key questions, reveal core assumptions, and evaluate alternatives—helping to clarify pathways and possibilities."

—David Bornstein, author of *How To Change The World* and the *New York Times* "Fixes" Column

"Effective problem-solving in our daily lives requires orderly thinking. Cheryl Einhorn shows us a way to do it in a short, clearly written book. Her lessons are organized around case studies that are free of jargon and to the point. In fact, her case studies are short novels that draw the reader into the dilemmas her characters face. They provide wonderful illustrations of how to go about making difficult decisions. Her book is a 'must read' those of us facing major decisions about our personal and professional futures."

—John Campbell, former United States Ambassador to Nigeria and currently the Ralph Bunche senior fellow for Africa policy studies at the Council on Foreign Relations

PROBLEM SOLVED

PROBLEM SOLVED

A Powerful System for
Making Complex Decisions With
Confidence and Conviction

Cheryl Strauss Einhorn

Foreword by Tony Blair

CAREER
PRESS
Wayne, NJ

PROBLEM SOLVED
Edited by Gina Schenck
Typeset by Diana Ghazzawi
Cover design by Rob Johnson/toprotype

Printed in the U.S.A.

To order this title, please call toll-free 1-800-CAREER-1 (NJ and Canada: 201-848-0310) to order using VISA or MasterCard, or for further information on books from Career Press.

The Career Press, Inc.
12 Parish Drive
Wayne, NJ 07470
www.careerpress.com

Library of Congress Cataloging-in-Publication Data

CIP Data Available Upon Request.

One day when I was a young girl, my mother went out and got her makeup done at a local department store makeup counter. When she returned, she asked my father how she looked. He replied, "Dear, when I look at you I see my fantasy, not the makeup you're wearing." She wondered aloud if that meant he didn't really look at her. Even as a little girl, I realized that it meant he saw her perfectly.

My mother was always the practical one who kept a set of encyclopedias in the car so we could read and learn even en route to the supermarket. My father's been the dreamer who saw and asked questions nobody else did.

This book is dedicated to both of my parents, who have taught me different ways of seeing.

Acknowledgments

As a young girl I loved mysteries, especially the notion of solving something, hunting for clues, and finding a trail where none was obvious. I grew up to be an investigative reporter since I couldn't be Trixie Belden. I taught factual sleuthing to many students at Columbia, never realizing that I was teaching a process and a way of thinking. Through time, it gestated and refined into a method: the AREA Method.

I still recall when I came up with the AREA acronym and who arrived at just that moment to hear about it: my dad. He'd come over for the weekly Sabbath celebration. It was perfect because he is a researcher *extraordinaire* and *Shabbat* is a time when we strategically stop each week to say thank you.

Of course, many other people were instrumental in discussing and working on this book with me.

Peter Lawrence, a former student, but now my co-teacher at Columbia and friend, was all-important in our conversations and work together.

Cathleen Barnhart, who once taught my kids and now has taught me not only about storytelling and writing but also about friendship.

To my agent Stacey Glick for believing in this book and in me, and for her guidance through the process to help it find a good home.

To other friends and colleagues who read the manuscript and shared their thoughtful, useful feedback: Dina Berrin, Tony Blair, David Bornstein, John Campbell, Jonathon Gruber, Liz Landau, Joe Platt, and Marc Skvirsky.

To John Christopher, who let me share his inspirational story, his research, and his good works, I'd like to donate half of all the proceeds from this book to your Oda Foundation.

And to David, I know that saying I love you is never saying enough, but it's a beginning.

For readers who would like to stay in touch, I look forward to hearing from you about how the AREA Method works for you. Please contact me through the areamethod.com website.

Disclaimer

All of the research in this book represents a snapshot in time. Websites and documents are routinely updated and information changes, so what John, Micah, Claudia, or Bill, or even I, found, may not be indicative of anyone else's experience now. All of the research and decisions were made at a moment in time by one person with one set of personal Critical Concepts. You, your Critical Concepts, and the information you find will be different.

Contents

Foreword

One of the fascinating aspects of leadership is the process of decision-making. And the challenge of doing it properly is the same in any walk of life—leading a company, a community, a country, or even a football team.

But of course in everyday life, we also make big decisions in how we lead our own lives: about what career move to make, where to live, how to handle family concerns and crises, how to identify our life's goals, and how to meet them effectively.

How do you get the best possible chance of making them correctly? This is the subject of Cheryl Einhorn's book. She believes that you can apply an analytical framework to decision-making which improves the possibility of a good outcome. I think it is a really interesting idea and the book makes it clear and simple to follow.

In essence, the method called AREA breaks down the process of making a decision, teaching you how to avoid bias and preconception which may be misconception, allowing you to define accurately the Critical Concepts at the core of the decision, which enable you to assess what is really the objective you seek to achieve and how.

It draws an analogy with the way a cheetah hunts. The key is the animal's ability to decelerate and pause, giving it the opportunity to turn and change direction where necessary to pursue its prey. In the same way, when taking a critical decision, she shows how at crucial moments it pays to slow down, to re-assess, and sometimes to switch course. She suggests a methodology as to how to do it.

The AREA Method is exemplified by reference to real case studies of real life—which university or program to choose or how to make the right care choice for elderly parents. But the significance of the AREA way of thinking is that it can be applied to anything from politics to business to creative art.

She shows how good decision-making is part imagination and part science. This excellent book shows how the science of decision-making can be applied and therefore the outcome made better. In today's world of complexity, that is a pretty useful guide!

—Tony Blair, former UK Prime Minister

How to Use This Book

Doing research—even focused, limited research—is messy. There's a wealth of information and details to keep track of. I suggest keeping all of your research organized in an AREA journal. Record all copies of your work and date each entry. By cataloguing your work and thoughts, you will not only have a record that you can refer back to as you move through the AREA process, but you will also prevent thesis creep, those pesky evolving hypotheses that make us feel that we have a rational reason to do something despite a change in circumstances. Your written records will also provide you with a roadmap for your research.

To dig deeper and share your own thoughts, join the AREA community by checking out my website, areamethod.com. There you will find further discussion about the method, related research, and articles, as well as how to post your own questions and decision-making experiences.

At many points I recommend making a strategic stop in your work and include a Cheetah Sheet, the graphic organizers that will help you build and hone the skills that you need to carry out the AREA Method. The sheets highlight sources of information, provide you with key questions that you will want to ask of the data you collect, and offer interpretation and analysis guidelines. They also provide you with checklists and exercises to help you effectively and efficiently conduct your research and hone your Critical Concepts. A full list of the Cheetah Sheets can be found in the Contents.

As you respond to the material in the Cheetah Sheets in your AREA journal, I encourage you to record both the questions that arise during the process and the answers you find. By keeping the journal, you'll be writing the story of your research and decision-making process. You'll sum up each "chapter" of your work—"A," "R," "E," and "A"—by consolidating your learning with one or more thesis statements. These statements sum up your research, your findings, and your analysis. The analysis is critical. It sums up the "So what?" of your research and points to the path forward, or the path back into the process. It may feel difficult or frustrating to stop at this point in your research, but the pause will make your research process better. Strategic deceleration in your information-gathering and processing builds agility and flexibility.

Cheetah Sheet

Turning Good Ideas Into Great Thinking

	THEORY / IDEA	PRACTICE / THINKING

A Absolute
Understand your target

1. Look at the numbers
2. Explore the website
3. Learn about leadership

R Relative
Research related sources

1. Map the industry
2. Review the literature
3. Reconcile narratives

E Exploration
Broaden your perspective

1. Identify good prospects
2. Craft great questions
3. Conduct interviews

Exploitation
Challenge assumptions

1. Consider rival hypotheses
2. Conduct pro/con exercise
3. Analyze future scenarios

A Analysis
Reduce uncertainty.
Make your decision.

1. Think about mistakes
2. Conduct a pre-mortem
3. **Come to conviction**

Navigating the Gray AREA

If you knew what you were doing it wouldn't be
called research.
—Albert Einstein

John Christopher, the founder of a Nepal-based charity called the
Oda Foundation, was on his way to breakfast during a family va-
cation in London on April 25, 2015, when he learned that a mas-
sive earthquake had struck Nepal, killing nearly 10,000 and injuring
more than double that number.

John had started the Oda Foundation, which provides basic
healthcare services to people in the rural village of Oda, Nepal,
less than two years earlier after volunteering at a school in nearby
Surkhet. He had chosen the remote village of Oda, a 16-hour flight,
drive, and hike from Nepal's capital of Kathmandu, because it had
a shortage of resources and John thought he could help. He figured
that by providing basic healthcare services—the leading causes of
death in Oda were diarrhea and childbirth—he could save a life for
as little as $2.23.

His efforts were met with immediate success. In his first year, on
a total budget of $25,000, he estimated he had saved roughly 40 lives,
making his little startup one of the most efficient healthcare founda-
tions in the world.

When John heard the news in London, he was relieved to learn
that his community was outside the earthquake's deadly range, and

his attention turned to a new urgent question: How could he quickly transform his on-the-ground team into a more useful health service provider for Nepal? How could he best serve the health needs of a country that suddenly looked very different from the country where he had operated for the past two years?

He laid out his options in his head. There were three different paths he could follow. Path One: Expand beyond his rural clinic by opening a new health clinic on a main road where his staff could easily service more patients. Path Two: Accept the Nepalese government's offer to partner with their existing health clinics to expand the government's treatment and care. Path Three: In a country with such treacherous terrain, invest in drones to drop and deliver medical kits around the country.

Which option should he choose? The strategies were very different from one another. How could he decide which course of action was the right one? He didn't want to rush to judgment, even though time was of the essence. How could he swiftly arrive at a well-reasoned and researched outcome to make an educated decision for a future that at first glance seemed so unpredictable?

John was faced with a high-stakes decision that would have a long-term impact on the well-being of his foundation and its reputation, a decision that needed to be made with incomplete information amid a volatile backdrop, in a changing environment with an urgent need for medical care.

That's the problem John came to me with just after the earthquake. We met just days before the tragedy, in the halls at Columbia University's Business School, where I was co-teaching a course in Advanced Investment Research. For this course, I was using and teaching a research and decision-making process that I'd developed called the "AREA Method," an acronym that gets its name from the perspectives it addresses. I realized AREA was applicable to John's problem.

As a journalist, teacher, consultant, mother, sister, wife, daughter, and friend, I've learned that there are few absolutes—and many gray areas. We each experience the world differently. I put together the AREA Method as a way to navigate gray areas and avoid those mental shortcuts that enable us to make small decisions easily but may impair our judgment when making big decisions. In short, I was searching for a better way to make big decisions.

In developing AREA, I realized that the process does much more than provide a research and decision-making roadmap; it makes your work *work* for you. It heightens your awareness to the motivations and incentives of others. It helps you avoid bias in your work and engage with people and problems more mindfully. Decision-making is about ideas, but ideas aren't enough. There is an important gap between having ideas and making good decisions about what to do with those ideas.

It can be messy and overwhelming to figure out how to solve big problems or make high-stakes decisions. Friends often asked me, "Where do you start? How do you know where to look for information and how to evaluate it? How can you feel confident that you are making a careful and thoroughly researched decision in such a volatile, uncertain world?" I believe the AREA Method will provide you with both the confidence and knowhow to do just that.

The AREA Method has worked for me professionally and for the countless students I've taught at both Columbia Business School and the Columbia University Graduate School of Journalism, as well as for a diverse mix of for-profit and not-for-profit clients that hire me for strategy consulting work. But the AREA Method has also changed my *thinking*. I have found that I'm applying the framework as a way to think about all sorts of personal and professional decisions.

The AREA process gets its name from the perspectives that it addresses: Absolute, Relative, Exploration and Exploitation, and

Analysis. The first "A" stands for "Absolute," which refers to primary, uninfluenced information from the sources at the center of your research and decision-making process. The "R" stands for "Relative," and refers to the perspectives of outsiders around your research subject. It is secondary information, or information that has been filtered through sources connected to your subject. The "E" stands for "Exploration" and "Exploitation," and they are the twin engines of creativity—one is about expanding your research breadth and the other is about depth. Exploration asks you to listen to other peoples' perspectives by developing sources and interviewing. Exploitation asks you to focus inward, on you as the decision-maker, to examine how you process information, examining and challenging your own assumptions and judgment. The second "A" stands for "Analysis," and synthesizes all of these perspectives, processing and interpreting the information you've collected. Each of these steps will be explained in detail in the chapters that follow.

Together the "A" and the "R" provide you with the tools necessary to create a framework for gathering and evaluating information. The latter part of the AREA Method, the "E" and the "A," provide detailed examination tools gleaned from experts in other fields such as investigative journalism, intelligence gathering, psychology, and medicine.

The AREA Method

AREA is a decision-making process focused on mining the insights and incentives of others to help you manage mental shortcuts. The steps build upon one another, radiating out from the center, and also serve as a feedback loop. The views and insights of other stakeholders are integrated until you fit them together.

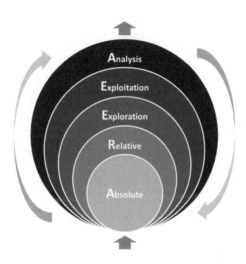

AREA helps you make smarter, better decisions by improving upon classic research and decision-making pedagogy in four important ways:

1. AREA recognizes that research is a fundamental part of decision-making.

2. AREA solves the problem of mental myopia—assumption, bias, and judgment in particular—through its construction as a perspective-taking process.

3. AREA addresses the critical component of timing so that you have time for calculated and directed

reflections that promote insight, that is, slowing down to speed up the efficacy of your work.

4.   AREA provides a clear, concise, and repeatable process that works as a feedback loop in part or in its entirety.

Advantages of the AREA Method

The AREA Method helps you bring greater CARE to making smarter, better decisions.

Craft Critical Concepts	• Your Critical Concepts focus your research and address the driving purpose behind your decision • Advantage: Keeps you focused on what matters the most.
Address biases	• We bring our assumptions and judgements to the way we view the world. • Advantage: AREA pre-empts and controls for our mental shortcuts.
Reveal perspectives	• Breaks down the research process into a series of easy-to-follow steps. • Advantage: Helps you make sense of the insights and incentives of others.
Extract learning	• Cheetah Pauses "slow down time" to accelerate your work—"strategic stops" in the research process. • Advantage: Chunk your learning to either forge ahead or loop back into the AREA process.

AREA recognizes that research is a fundamental part of decision-making

In reality, your ability to make a thoughtful decision is dependent upon the quality of the information you have. Therefore, you need a good research process to be an integral part of a decision-making framework. Currently, there are no methods out there that guide you through a research process with respect to making a decision at the end of it.

In fact, the current popular decision-making books and tools often lump the processes of "do research" or "evaluate your options" into a single step. AREA recognizes that *research* is an umbrella term for a whole series of tricky steps that need to be carefully navigated and thoughtfully completed. AREA breaks down the research so it is not a "black box." Instead, it's manageable and organized into an easy step-by-step logical progression.

You may shudder at the idea of doing research, thinking back to painful hours spent in your high school or college library, trying to stay awake as you plodded through musty, outdated books. But the task you face now—making an important personal or professional decision—isn't like the research process you followed in school; these high-stakes decisions are not closed cases. You're no longer studying something from the past; you're planning for an uncertain but important future: yours.

The AREA Method allows you to become your own expert in the ecosystem related to the decision you need to make. In that sense, it's more than a process that you apply—it's a muscle that you build and it can become second nature; it can be part of the frame you bring to the world.

AREA solves mental myopia through its construction as a perspective-taking process

Much has been written about how we are all prey to mental mistakes. Behavioral science research and books such as Robert Cialdini's *Influence* and Daniel Kahneman's *Thinking Fast and Slow* explain that we rely on faulty intuition and are swayed by authority and public sentiment, but they don't give us tools or techniques to overcome our flawed thinking. Instead, this new research explores the many ways that we allow biases, snap judgments, and assumptions to drive our decision-making. Although these pathways help us to make decisions quickly and easily, they impede our ability to think open-mindedly and thoroughly about complex problems. In other words, we know our thinking is flawed, but we don't know what to do about it. AREA gives us a framework to proactively manage these flaws.

AREA moves you from one vantage point to the next, isolating and categorizing information based on its source, enabling you to fully appreciate each perspective's point of view and the incentives that shape it.

Perspective-taking acknowledges that although you may think that you understand how to solve a particular problem, your understanding of that problem is most likely incomplete and different from how other key players see it. By walking in their shoes, you will better recognize other players' considerations and incentives. You may even come to understand the facts differently. But the method doesn't just look closely at what others are doing and perceiving; it also guides you to look inward by taking you through a series of self-assessment exercises. I learned about these exercises from other disciplines including medicine, investigative journalism, and intelligence-gathering. They point out flaws in our understanding of the research to highlight and help us catch—and correct—failures of data and failures of analysis.

AREA addresses the critical component of timing head-on

High-stakes decisions deserve time and attention, but we're in such a rush to reach a conclusion that we never take the time for deep reflection. We're already over-programmed, often answering emails late at night and waking to urgent texts. We struggle with the need to react when we also need to think. Yet when it comes to our future, we deserve the time needed for thoughtful reflection. Insight doesn't come from collecting information alone; it comes from brainwork, so AREA builds in what I call "Cheetah Pauses." Why the cheetah? Because the cheetah's prodigious hunting skills are not due to its speed. Rather, it's the animal's ability to *decelerate* quickly that makes it a fearsome hunter.

Cheetahs habitually run down their prey at speeds approaching 60 miles per hour, but are able to cut their speed by 9 miles per hour *in a single stride*, an advantage in hunting greater than being able to quickly accelerate. This allows the cheetah to make sharp turns, sideways jumps, and direction changes.

As cheetah researcher Alan Wilson explained in a 2013 *New York Times* article, *Cheetah's Secret Weapon: A Tight Turning Radius*, "The hunt is much more about maneuvering, about acceleration, about ducking and diving to capture the prey."

Similar to the cheetah's hunt, the AREA Method offers both stability and maneuverability; it doesn't consistently move forward. Instead, it benefits from calculated pauses and periods of thoughtful deceleration that will enable you to consolidate knowledge before accelerating again. The reason: A quality research and decision-making process is about depth, flexibility, and creativity.

The method's Cheetah Pauses work as strategic stops during and after each part of your research. They enable you to chunk your learning, prevent you from going off course, and provide a clear record of your work at each stage. But most importantly, they will help you hone in on the motivation for making your high-stakes decision and identify what is most critical to *you* in the outcome. These are what I call "Critical Concepts." They get at the driving purpose behind your decision.

Critical Concepts (CCs) are the one, two, or three things that really matter to you. They answer the question "What am I really solving for?" There is no single answer. Critical Concepts are going to vary from person to person. Different decision-makers will have different time horizons in which to make their decisions, different personalities, and different goals. Two people looking at the same data may have different CCs and may make entirely different decisions.

As you move through the AREA Method, the pauses will help you continually refine and re-articulate your CCs based upon what you learn and synthesize from your research. They are an integral part of the AREA process. The goal of the CCs is to ensure you are laser-focused on making a decision that uniquely addresses the essence of what you really need to resolve. Taking the time to identify what's critical to you—your CCs—is the foundation to my analytical method.

You don't need lots of money or resources to make a good decision, but you do need good methodology and a clear sense of what you want out of your decision. Whether you're making a critical professional or personal decision, the AREA Method is an equitable tool that gives you a step-by-step framework that focuses your work and thinking on Critical Concepts.

AREA provides a clear, concise, and repeatable process that works as a feedback loop

Not all investigations are linear, nor should they be. At times you need to be driven back into earlier steps to do more work, collect more data, or conduct further analysis.

Still, while every hunt a cheetah undertakes is different, an experienced hunter learns from past hunts and uses these lessons to make them more effective. The same is true for making decisions about ideas, opportunities, or problems. A solid research and decision-making process should be explicit, improvable, flexible, and, above all, repeatable. The process should not start and stop with each idea, opportunity, or problem, but should build from each investigation to the next, becoming more refined as you gain experience.

Rest assured that refining your AREA process does not mean narrowing your thinking. It's the opposite. The idea behind AREA is to continually create cognitive space to openly receive new data inputs so that you gain insight from others and from disconfirming data.

For example, political pundits forecast for a living, and one of the most important predictions they make is about who will be each party's presidential nominee. Their expectations about the contenders often both mirror and influence voters, and help candidates get screen time and media coverage. Yet, in the fall of 2015, every political pundit dismissed Donald Trump as a viable candidate for the Republican Party's presidential nomination. They focused on his lack of experience and divisiveness, making him unqualified in the eyes of the Republican leadership. Two biases (at least) were at play here: Projection Bias, where we assume that others believe as we do, and Authority Bias, where we defer to authority figures, and they overwhelmed the experts' ability to see disconfirming data. State by state, voters went to the ballot box and told the pundits they were wrong, but the pundits didn't listen. They didn't get beyond their own perspective and they got the outcome wrong. They missed the mood of the country and the rising populist anger Donald Trump tapped into.

Regardless of whether you are new to making high-stakes decisions or do it for a living, you will benefit from having a framework that enables you to spot and analyze information in a strategically open-minded way.

At its heart, the AREA process of perspective-taking is meant to help you check your ego, enable you to better judge the incentives of others, and explore a situation more objectively. In so doing, it builds both self-awareness and empathy. As AREA becomes second nature, it can be part of the frame you bring to the world around you. And in so doing, it may allow you to live your life more mindfully and enable you to take advantage of your ideas. With the right framework, the right approach to decision-making—*the right process*—you can turn good ideas into great thinking. It's a simple yet powerful equation:

A Good Process + Good Information = Great Decisions

Cognitive Biases and AREA Method Remedies

Mental short cuts are critical for our well-being. They remind us of what we know, and help us process information quickly. They allow us to move through our day without being continually overwhelmed by the decisions we have to make. But in order to make decisions quickly, without continued mental effort, these decision shortcuts necessarily become biases, or in other words, snap judgments. Yet these same cognitive biases limit us as objective thinkers and observers. When we face high-stakes decisions, we don't want to use the same old worn pathways. We want to be more expansive in our thinking and open new channels to exercise true objectivity and creativity.

There are many good articles and books on the topic of cognitive biases and flawed thinking. Two of my favorites are Berkshire Hathaway Vice-Chairman Charlie Munger's 1995 speech at Harvard University, "The Psychology of Human Misjudgment," and Robert Cialdini's book *Influence*.

The following list contains common cognitive biases that can impede good decision-making but that the AREA Method can help you overcome. The list starts with the name of the bias, along with its significance and an example of how it may impede clear thinking. Underneath that information, the text explains how the AREA Method tackles this specific bias and directs you to the chapter in which you can find the solution.

The AREA Method was created to provide an easy to follow and flexible process that breaks down decision-making into discrete pieces; you may follow all of it, or pick and choose the pieces that you feel will best resolve your decision. I encourage you to read the book all the way through before beginning your work so that you understand the comprehensive process and plan your time more effectively when you do begin research.

The planning fallacy

The planning fallacy is our tendency to underestimate the time, costs, and risks of completing a task, even though we've previously experienced similar tasks. Time management is a significant issue in research and decision-making. We may miss out on an opportunity because we've underestimated how long it takes us to conduct our research. The AREA Method is designed to reduce planning fallacy in two ways:

1. The Cheetah Sheets let you know how much to wring out of each part of the research process, which aids in assessing the time that it will take to complete each section.

2. By repeating a consistent process, you will reduce the likelihood of poorly planning your time.

Confirmation bias

The confirmation bias refers to a form of selective thinking in which we seek out and overvalue information that confirms our existing beliefs, while neglecting or undervaluing information that is contradictory to our existing beliefs. It is related to commitment and consistency bias where we behave in a way that validates our prior actions. It is also related to the incentive bias where we adapt our views to what benefits us. A confirmation bias may lead us to interpret information falsely because it conflicts with our prior views and beliefs. Confirmation biases can lead to overconfidence in personal beliefs, even in the face of contrary evidence. In business and in our personal lives, it can lead to extremely poor (and costly) decisions.

The AREA Method was created specifically to slow our disposition to make assumptions and pass judgment while enabling us to better assess the incentives of others.

The AREA Method is designed to reduce confirmation bias in the following ways:

1. In the **Exploration** chapter, you will learn to craft objective questions.

2. In the **Exploitation** chapter, both the Competing Alternative Hypotheses exercise and the Pro/Con exercise will help to prevent this bias.

3. In the **Analysis** chapter, the discussion about the Rule of Three and the Pre-Mortem exercise both tackle confirmation bias.

Optimism bias

This is a bias in which someone's subjective confidence in their judgments, or in the judgments of others, is reliably greater than their objective accuracy. For example, we are only correct about 80 percent of the time when we are "99 percent sure."

The AREA Method is designed to reduce optimism bias in the following ways:

1. In the **Absolute** chapter, the guidance to read numbers before narrative will counter this bias.

2. In **Exploitation**, the Pro/Con and Scenario Analysis exercises address it.

3. In **Analysis**, the Pre-Mortem exercise will help you to counter this bias.

Projection bias

Without meaning to, we tend to project our thoughts and beliefs on to others and assume that they are wired the same way we are. This can lead to "false consensus bias," which not only assumes that other people think like we do, but that they reach the same conclusions that we have reached. In short, this bias creates a false consensus or sense of confidence. For example, if we like a product, we will assume other people like it as much as we do. By following the AREA Method, you will be using a source-based methodology that is structured to heighten your awareness of your own thinking while focusing clearly on other people's viewpoints.

The AREA Method is designed to reduce projection bias in the following ways:

1. In the **Exploitation** chapter, Competing Alternative Hypotheses, Pro/Con, and Scenario Analysis exercises control this bias.

2. In the **Analysis** chapter, the Pre-Mortem exercise addresses it.

Social proof

We tend to think and believe what the people around us think and believe. We see ourselves as individuals but we actually run in herds—large or small, bullish or bearish. The AREA Method provides a natural defense against this bias because it is a structured process and it encourages you to do your own work, broken down into discrete and manageable research pieces. With AREA, you are always aware of the source(s) of your information and focused on their incentives and your own.

The AREA Method is designed to reduce social proof in the following ways:

1. In **Exploration**, you will develop new sources of information and learn how to ask objective questions.

2. In **Exploitation**, the Competing Hypothesis exercise structures how we analyze data to avoid bias. The Pro/Con exercise will also battle this bias.

3. In **Analysis**, the Checklists discussion will help you think about crafting lists to check and challenge your thinking and information.

Salience bias

Salience bias refers to the tendency to overestimate evidence that is recent or vivid. For example, people greatly overestimate murder as a cause of death when actually murder isn't even among the top 15 causes of death in the United States. There are more than 10 times as many deaths from heart disease (the leading cause of death) than murder. By using the AREA Method, you will be focused on your cognitive shortcuts.

The AREA Method is designed to reduce salience bias in the following ways:

1. In **Exploitation**, exercises like Competing Alternative Hypotheses systematically ensures you consider all of your information. Visual Mapping and Scenario Analysis will also address this bias by putting your evidence into context.

2. In **Analysis**, the section on Thinking About Mistakes as well as the Checklist exercise will challenge you to focus on significant issues, as opposed to salient ones.

Narrative bias

We prefer stories—narratives—to data. Narratives are crucial to how we make sense of reality. They help us to explain, understand, and interpret the world around us. They also give us a frame of reference we can use to remember the concepts we take them to represent. However, our inherent preference of narrative over data often limits our understanding of complicated situations. For example, a good story can sell almost anything.

The AREA Method is designed to reduce narrative bias in the following ways:

1. Beginning with numbers and data in the **Absolute** phase, the AREA Method is structured specifically to counter this bias.

2. The Cheetah Pauses encourage you to distill and analyze information.

3. In **Exploitation**, Scenario Analysis deals with this bias, directing you to create multiple narratives for your research target's Critical Concepts, enabling you to use story-telling as a strength instead of a weakness.

Loss aversion

Empirical estimates find that losses are felt almost two-and-a-half times as strongly as gains. An example is that if we have recently lost money in an investment, we might be unlikely to make similar investments in the future.

The AREA Method is designed to reduce loss aversion in the following ways:

1. In **Exploitation**, exercises like Competing Alternative Hypotheses ask you to withhold judgment and consider scenarios that at first might not appear likely. Pro/Con

and Scenario Analysis also asks you to project possible outcomes.

2. In **Analysis,** the Pre-Mortem exercise will guide you to consider failure *before* you make the decision to further battle this bias. You'll develop a plan to counteract failure and boost your confidence that your decision is set up to succeed.

Relativity bias

The relativity bias inhibits our ability to objectively assess information based upon an over-dependence on comparisons. For example, when given a choice, we tend to pick the middle option: not too pricey, not too cheap.

The AREA Method is designed to reduce relativity bias in the following ways:

1. In **Exploitation**, the Pro/Con exercise and the Competing Alternative Hypothesis counters this bias.

2. In **Analysis,** the Pre-Mortem exercise will focus on what could go wrong with comparisons and how to prevent it from happening.

Authority bias

This bias refers to our natural inclination to follow and to believe in authority figures. For example, Nike pays Rory McIlroy millions of dollars to wear the company's logo betting that consumers will follow his lead.

The AREA Method is designed to reduce authority bias in the following way: The AREA Method separates **Absolute** and **Relative** information to counter this bias. If the information we receive from an authority figure conflicts with information we have received from another source, we will identify the dissonance.

Liking bias

If you like someone or something, you will interpret data in their favor. We tend to like people who are like us, or have qualities that we admire. For example, you might be inclined to favor a candidate who went to your alma mater. This bias is closely related to the reciprocity bias in which we want to reciprocate a favor that someone has done for us. The AREA Method is designed to reduce liking bias in the following ways:

1. The AREA Method separates **Absolute** information from information that you receive from other people, such as those in the **Relative** and **Exploration** phase.

2. In **Exploitation**, the Competing Alternative Hypotheses, Pro/Con, and Scenario Analysis exercises will help you separate and objectively analyze your data and your hypotheses.

Scarcity

We tend to covet things we believe are scarce, sometimes irrationally. For example, during the real estate bubble, investors became concerned that only a limited amount of land was available to be developed with no real evidence that this was the case.

The AREA Method is designed to reduce scarcity bias in the following ways:

1. The AREA Method's close focus on checking our thinking.

2. In **Exploitation**, the Competing Alternative Hypotheses, Visual Map, and Scenario Analysis exercises address how we approach and evaluate discrete data points in context.

3. In **Analysis**, the Pre-Mortem addresses the ways that your decision might fail.

These biases are all difficult to counter, but they are even more powerful when they are combined. If one bias is present, you might be able to recognize it, but if several biases are at work at the same time, it is much harder. Berkshire Hathaway's Munger calls this the "Lollapalooza effect." The AREA Method controls all of these biases and other decision-making blind spots by inhabiting the perspective of one source of information at a time. Throughout the book, I provide you with tools called "Cheetah Sheets" to organize your data collection and your thinking because they encourage you to pause, think strategically and creatively, and refine your hunt for the right decision, just like a cheetah.

AREA at Work

To illustrate the AREA Method, I've chosen four different kinds of high-stakes decisions—two professional decisions and two personal ones—that I'll discuss throughout the book. We'll learn more about John Christopher's classic business decision: What strategy should he use to quickly grow his organization? And we'll follow Claudia who, mid-way through her career as an advertising executive, wanted to switch careers before she was downsized out of a shrinking and fragmented field. She wanted to be in a growth industry with more stability but was unsure which of two very different paths—nursing school or computer programming—to follow.

We will also examine an increasingly common and very emotional personal decision when we meet Bill, who had to decide what kind of move he should help his aging parents make. Bill felt that his parents couldn't manage the house and the steep driveway in their multistory home where they'd raised their family. Bill needed to decide whether to encourage them to downsize into an intermediate home or to go directly into a housing facility that offered a continuum of care for the elderly.

Finally, we will follow the story of Micah, a high-school senior, who had to decide between two very different college acceptance packages in a few short weeks. (To see a summary of the decision-makers' AREA process and Critical Concepts turn to Appendix A.)

The unifying theme of these decisions is that they are issues that are important enough to merit a research process and difficult enough to benefit from one. Life is filled with uncertainty, but we don't want to let it hobble us, and frankly we don't want to gamble with our future either. We also don't want to rely on hope or "intuition" alone. Instead, we want a proactive way to work with, and work through, ambiguity to make thoughtful high-conviction decisions *despite* our uncertain and volatile world.

John, for example, says the AREA Method was transformational in not only helping him make an educated, informed decision about which growth strategy to pursue, but also in accelerating his fundraising in a way that he had not anticipated. During the nearly two years John's foundation had been operational before the earthquake, he had raised $90,000. After completing the AREA Method, he was able to reach out to new donors with a clear, concise, and cogent story backed by evidence for what he wanted to do and how and why his team was likely to succeed. In *two months*, June and July 2015, while I was writing this book, John raised more than $150,000. John described his experience with the AREA Method as such:

> I really didn't have a lot of structure for how I conducted research before. I made spreadsheets and phone calls and relied upon my own experience. The AREA Method has been game-changing. It's given me a disciplined approach to problem-solving and a way to make sure that I consider the incentives and biases of others. It also taught me a host of new creative ways to identify sources and information. It provided practical training for how to conduct interviews so

that I'd ask the right questions to the right people to get targeted, actionable information.

The Method also introduced John to interpretation and analysis tools to evaluate his work, ascribe value to it, and come to a final decision with conviction. John not only had a path forward, but by following the AREA Method, he also had a record of his thinking about his work at critical junctures that would inform future decisions. He learned how to focus on other peoples' perspectives and to identify and temper his own bias and judgments. Before this point, John had never paused and tried to see things from the Nepali people's perspective, even though he'd been working with them for years. However, as he delved into their understanding of Nepal's healthcare system in his AREA research process, he added this insight into the likelihood of succeeding with each of his growth options.

In addition, the AREA Method work improved John's analysis and understanding of his current clinic's work. He recognized that he could expect greater economic and social volatility ahead for Nepal as the country sorted out its road to recovery after the earthquake, and that times of improvement might not necessarily point to a sign of stability. Nonetheless, with AREA, he realized that he was not frozen in indecision; despite the uncertainty, AREA gave him a way to make big decisions that could lead to a successful research outcome.

We all know that, at times, even a good process may have a poor outcome. You might have bad luck or dumb luck; sometimes you get your just desserts and sometimes your just rewards. I believe that in applying the AREA Method, you will gain the skills, tools, and confidence necessary to improve and enhance your research and decision-making process.

Value-added research, as this process applies it, is a step to developing a comprehensive, objective analysis of a problem that focuses not just on prudent information collection, but on analyzing the information in a rigorous, unbiased manner. The goal is to feel that, in completing the AREA Method, you have both comfort and conviction to make a well-informed, thoughtful decision.

Researchers tell us that we make about 30,000 decisions a day, everything from which part of the toothpaste tube to squeeze to whether you should have a late-night snack, and we don't need the AREA Method for those daily decisions. Life's big decisions, however, have big consequences. This book and method will take you through a step-by-step analytic process to make those big decisions in a mindful way that overcomes potential errors and common biases.

At the end of this process, you will have a thoughtful, well-researched, analytically supported decision. And, as you'll see in the upcoming pages, it's an extraordinary thing to get a big decision right. For John, it meant more than growing his charity; it meant saving lives. For Micah, it meant that he was starting college with a real plan for his future and an understanding of who he was as a student and learner. Advertising executive Claudia knew she was ready to undertake a difficult and costly life change, but the AREA Method helped her see what uncertainty she was willing to tolerate and what uncertainty she wasn't. For Bill, he went in thinking he'd find a one-stop solution that he could convince his parents would be the right one, but instead they all came together with a solution that Bill initially hadn't seen.

Now it's your turn.

There is no one right way to conduct research and make decisions, just as there is no one right way to eat an ice cream cone. While I lay out a clear order of operations and many research steps, the AREA process does not have to be applied as a whole. I encourage you to read through the book and understand all of the steps. However, once you've done that, feel free to choose the steps that resonate with you and that are most relevant to the decision you need to make.

The book can be used like a workbook long after an initial read. Refer to the Contents to find a list of the Cheetah Sheets, which will take you to sections of the AREA Method that you would like to use. You now have useful lists of suggested sources of information and questions to consider as you collect, analyze, and synthesize the data related to your decision.

Look at the different tools and methods I describe as suggestions and feel free to refine your research and decision-making approach however it feels best to you. But keep in mind: by pushing yourself to do research and analysis out of your comfort zone, you will push your thinking in constructive ways.

The AREA process has worked for me, for the clients in my consulting work, and in my classrooms for countless students throughout the years, breaking down the daunting task of research and decision-making into a more satisfying and manageable task. To read more about how I've used the Method and how it influences my thinking, check out my website and blog at areamethod.com.

At its core, there are two kinds of learning: knowledge and skill. The AREA Method is a skill. I will explain it and teach it to you, and by simply using it you will get better, improve, and make it your own. We can't control our luck, but we can control our process and, in doing so, make smarter, better decisions.

Research Edges and Pitfalls

Like many of his friends, John took a job in the financial industry after college. But his mother's unexpected death the year after he graduated changed his outlook; he wanted to do something meaningful that would directly help people. So after two years, he quit his finance job and went to Nepal. There, he volunteered at a rural school in Surkhet that served orphaned children and began to think about opening his own charity in nearby Oda.

"I felt that there was a real need for an orphanage and a school in Oda," John recalls. However, one day while he was working on the orphanage idea, John was approached by a man carrying his sick 10-year old daughter on his back. The man said he'd walked for three hours to see John, explaining that he'd heard John had helped other sick kids. The girl had a high fever and diarrhea. Her eyes were rolled back in her head and she was sweating, crying, and unable to walk. John gave her a basic antibiotic and fluids to make her comfortable and a place to sleep. The next day her fever broke and the diarrhea subsided. That night she smiled at John, said thank you in Nepali, and walked out of John's hut with her father. The cost of the treatment was $3.00. "I realized that even though I was not a doctor, I could make a difference," he says. "I could raise three dollars and find medical professionals. I didn't intend to set up an organization that provided healthcare. But I could see that kids were missing school and couldn't learn because of basic health issues like malnutrition and diarrhea. I had to take care of those issues before anything else could happen."

It wasn't only children who were affected. Nepalese of all ages were dying from conditions that would be easily treated, even cured, in the United States and other developed nations. John believed that by providing some basic healthcare and education, he could change that. And so he founded the Oda Foundation, a free-standing health clinic staffed with medical assistants and other volunteers.

At the time of the April 2015 earthquake, Oda's health clinic was serving about 1,000 patients a month, addressing a broad range of health problems including acute respiratory infections, typhoid fever, and trauma from common accidents and injuries. Oda was also conducting small education seminars, such as one focused on keeping teenage girls in school by providing education about, and hygiene products for, menstruation.

John quickly saw that his foundation could make a real difference. Between the time it opened its doors on December 12, 2013, and the end of 2014, Oda served about 25,000 of the addressable area's approximately 50,000 residents. The number of easily preventable deaths dropped from 50 in 2013 to zero in 2014 and the menstrual hygiene education campaign reduced school absences in the village by about 70 percent. When the earthquake struck in April 2015, John realized that Oda had an opportunity to quickly expand its services and help more people. But what type of expansion would be best for Oda, for John, and for the people of Nepal? Which of his three options would best allow Oda to save lives most effectively and efficiently? Each of the options held promise and peril for his organization. Each would fundamentally change its nature.

If he followed Option 1, opening a single roadside primary care clinic, Oda would be duplicating the care and education that it was providing in the village of Oda at a second location, but for a larger patient population. Oda would remain a direct service organization. It was the most limited option in scope, but gave Oda the greatest amount of control over administering care to patients.

In Option 2, if Oda partnered with Nepal's government healthcare system to offer education and training to the government's staff who manned a chain of clinics, he'd be turning Oda into an education and training organization. It would give Oda the broadest distribution network, but it was a train-the-trainer model. Oda's staff would teach government workers to deliver more primary care services, but the government's staff had a problematic reputation, including a tendency for absenteeism.

In Option 3, if Oda chose to deliver medicine and other medical supplies via drones to reach remote populations and clinics, Oda would be able to skirt Nepal's treacherous terrain to reach a much wider geographic area, but the decision would also change the nature of the organization into a medical supply organization. Did John want to do that? And if he chose this option, who would receive the kits, and how might Oda ensure that the contents were used properly?

The decision would dictate the direction of John's organization for the next several years. A failure could hurt Oda's credibility with its donors and stunt the organization's growth. Success would improve credibility and provide a platform for growth. This was a high-stakes decision that had consequences for John both professionally and personally. It was a turning point that required a carefully made decision. What's more, John didn't want to judge his options; he wanted to methodically gather information that would help him avoid pitfalls and develop an edge in making a well-reasoned, thoughtful decision that had a good chance of being successful.

That's one of the benefits as the AREA Method applies it; it helps you to be mindful of the edges and pitfalls in your research world. Some research is easy to do; the information is accessible, plentiful, and clear. Other research is cumbersome and tricky. The information may be opaque or insufficient. Recognizing where things may be working for you (where you have an edge) and where you may be at a disadvantage (facing a potential pitfall) can make the process more effective and efficient for you, even before you start. That way, you may think about how to counter your weaknesses and capitalize on your strengths.

To do that, consider the four ways you can frame your research. In so doing, you are, of course, making an assumption about how easy or difficult parts of the process may be. These four frames are Behavioral, Informational, Analytical, and/or Structural. Together they spell out BIAS.

Therefore, thinking about how to frame your edges and pitfalls asks you to think again about your BIAS, namely the assumptions you have about how it will all go. How do they apply to your situation? By confronting your expectations, you will also be managing for problematic mental short cuts.

- **Behavioral:** This frame is about paying attention and controlling your biases so that they don't negatively influence your behavior.
- **Informational:** This frame is about getting the right data. To effectively make a good decision, you need to have all of the pertinent facts in place.
- **Analytical:** This frame is about distilling and synthesizing your data to reach the right conclusions once you've collected the right data.
- **Structural:** This frame is about the opportunities and limitations of your environment. It gets at flexibility and timing. Are you in the right place at the right time, or might your decision be constrained by a deadline whereas others may be made under less pressure? John found himself with a giant structural edge in Nepal because his charity was one of the few health organizations already on the ground when the earthquake struck. "We were able to meet Operation USA when they landed in Kathmandu," says John. It gave his tiny charity a spotlight "and that made a huge difference."

The AREA process is structured so that you can identify your edges and pitfalls. All four are symbiotic, are meant to help you think about framing your work, and point toward areas where you need to know and do more.

AREA recognizes that researching and making high-stakes decisions is much more akin to playing a poker hand than it is to either your everyday decisions or your long-ago school research assignments. You're in the game to win, but so is everyone else at the table. How do you increase your odds of winning—of choosing the best path forward? You've got incomplete information, and the future will change in some ways you can predict and many you can't. But as the pros at the poker table will tell you (unless they're playing against you), there's information you can gather to give you better odds—and even an edge—in playing the hand you are dealt. The pros know they don't have to know *everything* because they only have to focus on what hands their cards can beat.

As you begin your research, you will want to think like a poker pro. What are the outcomes that matter for you in this game? You don't have to think about all hands. In fact, that would be distracting and counterproductive. Every poker player has a set of skills but they start each hand fresh, figuring out what's critical for that hand. The same will be true for you as a decision-maker as you develop your decision's Critical Concepts (CCs). As they say in poker, that's where you're "pot-committed." You've got chips on the table and a vested interest. The game is highly personal, subjective, and specific to your situation.

Here are two brief examples of the way CCs are integral to the AREA process:

1. High school seniors Micah and Kyle applied to colleges as pre-med majors. Both were deciding between two very different schools. Micah knew he wanted to pursue medicine, and had already spent a summer working in a medical lab doing research. He was specifically interested in academic medicine and imagined pursuing a fellowship or additional research training after medical school and residency. He was deciding between the University of Pittsburgh, where he'd been offered a full scholarship, and Johns Hopkins University, which had not offered any financial assistance.

   However, for Micah, an only child of two professional parents, the sizable cost difference between his two choices was not his primary CC. Micah and his parents were concerned with Micah receiving an undergraduate education that would set him up for the specific kind of medical career he envisioned. Equally important CCs for Micah were the accessibility of undergraduate research opportunities, medical school acceptance rates, and the selectivity of the medical schools each undergraduate institution was getting their students into.

Kyle was one of four children deciding between a free ride at the University of Pittsburgh and limited aid at Johns Hopkins. Kyle wanted to be a family practice doctor and had to fund medical school on his own. For Kyle, the cost of his undergraduate options was the overriding Critical Concept.

2. As Bill began his Absolute research phase, his friend Carol raved about the fabulous continuing care facility her parents had just moved into, about an hour away from the town where Bill and his parents lived. Carol encouraged Bill to check out the facility, but Bill knew his parents weren't the social butterflies that Carol's parents were. His parents' social interactions tended to be primarily with family and a few longtime friends. For Bill and his parents, a facility's busy and varied social calendar was not a Critical Concept, but staying near friends, family, and medical care providers they already had was much more important than exciting new social opportunities.

In my experience, for most decisions, although there are typically numerous relevant and material data points, only a few factors are critical to the outcome. For instance, in late 2011, a friend who is a jeweler considered selling a new line of jewelry made by a Danish company called Pandora. The company sold charm bracelets that had become popular but when he took a closer look at Pandora, he noticed that growth had flattened.

In response to missed growth projections, he noted that Pandora's stock price dropped by 80 percent as analysts worried the bracelets might be a fad and the company could shrink as quickly as it had grown. At this point, there was a wealth of information about the company, but almost all the information—the rate of inventory turnover, trends in input pricing, prospects for expanding their store base, and so on—was irrelevant to identifying greater certainty about future sales success. All that really mattered was whether or not the business was a fad.

The jeweler's research focused on determining whether charm bracelets were a fad. He called third-party retailers to understand the context of slowing customer purchases and the level of ongoing customer interest, analyzed resale channels to determine the extent to which bracelet owners were dumping previously purchased jewelry, measured Pandora-related Internet activity to gauge ongoing consumer engagement patterns, and interviewed industry veterans to understand the composition of historical fads.

Ultimately, his AREA research concluded that the slowdown in sales was concentrated in a few non-core items, and consumer interest was still robust; Pandora's success wasn't a short-term fad. The jeweler developed an informational edge on the one issue that truly mattered, and the result was a successful and very profitable decision to sell Pandora's bracelets and charms.

The goal of the AREA research process is not to be the most knowledgeable person about everything related to your research topic. In my experience, focusing on the 10th, 11th, and 12th Critical Concept is often more of a distraction. Your goal is to hone in on and creatively and intensively research the two or three CCs that will determine the success or failure of your decision so that you become knowledgeable about what really matters. To me, that's the foundation of practical and actionable research.

I will emphasize again: Open-ended research is not terribly productive. It's not only time consuming, but can feel overwhelming and ultimately counterproductive. The AREA process recognizes this and asks you to carefully determine your CCs. *What matters to you?* Use the answer to shape and frame your research process. It will make a difference between a frustrating, unhelpful process and a life changing affirmation that comes from a decision well made.

2

AREA = A: Absolute

We don't see things as they are. We see them as we are.

—Anais Nin

The AREA Method is constructed to help you make your unique high-stakes decision, but it does this in part by asking you to step outside of yourself and think from other people's perspectives. This may seem counterintuitive. After all, you're trying to figure out what matters to you. Why care about what matters to others?

By focusing on others' motivations and incentives, you will not only better understand their behavior, but also reflect a mirror back to how you are thinking, feeling, and acting. This perspective-taking helps you move from bias to objectivity and relates decision-making with behavior—both other stakeholders' and your own. By standing in someone else's perspective, you are also better able to grasp your own.

The first "A" in AREA stands for Absolute information, meaning information that represents the perspective closest to the entity or entities at the core of your decision. It is primary source information, unfiltered by outside, secondary sources.

It seems basic, but when you are researching something, sometimes the most valuable information comes from the subject at the center of the research process itself. For example, a few years ago I noticed a lot of donation cans with pictures of starving dogs popping up in my neighborhood stores. Instinctively, I placed change in these cans to help the poor, skinny dogs. But where was the money actually going? And what kind of oversight or verification existed for these kinds of charitable organizations?

I pitched my then-editors at *Inside Edition*, a syndicated television show, on an investigation into canister-collection charities, and promptly began to research the charity behind the skinny-dog photos. In the end, the 990 charity tax form disclosed that no money went to feeding dogs. The management kept most of the money to fund their own salaries; the rest went to neutering dogs. From the dogs' perspective, this difference was quite substantial.

Identifying Your Absolute Target

Every personal decision—whether it's about which college to attend or whether to move your aging parents to a nursing home—is impacted by a business or organization. As an individual, you will make a better decision if you are comfortable and familiar with this entity at the center of your research decision: your Absolute target.

So what would that mean for Bill, Claudia, or Micah? Bill needed Absolute information from the retirement and continuing care facilities he investigated for his parents. These were his Absolute targets. Claudia's Absolute targets were from the two career paths she compared—computer programming and nursing. She wanted to look at both the schools and programs where she could receive training and at potential employers in both fields, especially those that recruited at the schools she considered. Claudia also wanted to gather salary information for both paths. Micah's Absolute targets were the two universities he was deciding between.

The uniting factor between John, Bill, Micah, and Claudia is that in order to make their high-stakes decisions, they benefitted from better understanding the organizations and the costs that were at the center of the decisions they were trying to make. All of the decision-makers, as you just read, targeted several organizations and you may need to do so too. "Target" doesn't always mean only one entity. Bill initially settled on researching seven targets while Micah had two.

By first looking at the information directly from your Absolute target, you will also begin to understand how the target wants to be seen and how it would like others to interpret its results and prospects. You won't taint your impression of the decision or issue with outside or relative-source information. The goal is to gather information from this close-up on the target so that you have a foundation for comparison of the target's version of events versus those of other sources of information, making it easier to spot red flags or conflicts between the narratives later on. These conflicts help you identify and ferret out incentives and other hidden information that may impact your ability to make an educated and successful decision.

The first Cheetah Sheet provides you with a list of questions. These questions are guides for where and how to start your research and what questions to ask of the data you collect so that your work stays focused and productive. Feel free to personalize them by changing and adding questions as they pertain to your specific decision.

Cheetah Sheet 1: Getting to Know Your Target

1. What are your critical entities and your Absolute targets? Why?

2. Who are the critical people at those entities? What is their involvement and impact?

3. What does it mean as it relates to your decision?

Write out the answers in your AREA journal. Compose a list of unanswered questions for further study and make a list of sources you can go to for answers.

Numerical Data

Once you've identified your Absolute targets, begin your research by looking at the kind of numerical data they provide. All high-stakes decisions have numbers involved. Many have a financial or economic ramification to them. Although not all high-stakes decisions should be made based upon numbers, it's useful to know what numerical data your target makes available. How your target conveys its numerical data can tell you a lot about how the entity views itself and wants to be understood by others.

For almost all of us, research begins on the computer. To get your numbers, you'll go to your target's website. But stay focused on finding your target's relevant numerical data even though it may seem enticing to browse the whole site. You'll get to websites later in your Absolute work, but by beginning with the numbers, you can get a sense of your Absolute target in the most uninfluenced way. You'll strip away the noise of whatever hype there might be around your target or any emotional impression the target wants you to have.

Before you read anything else, the numbers will also enable you to build your own internal compass about the target, even if you're not a "numbers person." If you've balanced a checkbook or figured out the tip on a restaurant check, you've looked at numbers.

Reading and analyzing the numbers first keeps you from assuming that whatever your Absolute target says is backed up by its data. I have often found that a careful reading of the data opens up interpretations not included in the target's written analysis. You'll be better able to think about what your target says if you have first come to some conviction yourself.

If there is a publicly traded company that makes the goods or provides the service that you are interested in, you may want to look at the company's charts and tables from its Securities & Exchange Commission filings. You may not want or need to go this in-depth, but these are publicly available documents that can be obtained by a simple online search. Most organizations publish data directly, or file data with regulators.

To recap, the purpose of limiting your initial focus to the numbers is fourfold. First, it enables you to see your Absolute target as objectively and as uninfluenced as possible. Second, it recognizes that organizations, or entities, present data on what they consider to be their main issues. Reading the numbers first quickly highlights what the entity considers most critical beyond what it is obligated to disclose. Third, it enables you to consider whether the data is relevant and clear. For example, if a charity says it provides 100 meals, that doesn't tell you how many people queued up for meals. The data is not clear and we can't tell if it is relevant. And fourth, you're more likely to better examine your Absolute target's conclusions and interpretations of their numbers having first arrived at your own.

Cheetah Sheet 2: Just the Numbers

1. What kind of numerical data is available?

2. Does the numerical data make sense?
   a. Does it seem reasonable?
   b. Is there a connection between, or among, the data?

3. Are the numbers complete? Are they readable without a narrative?

4. Are they labeled and explained? If they are hard to understand, you've already exposed an inadequacy. If the numbers don't make sense, the story might not either.

5. What is the story that the numbers' charts and tables tell about your target?

6. Consider whether there are possible calculations that can help you derive value. For example, Bill might want to consider a ratio of staff members to residents when looking at continuing care facilities.

7. What is the significance for the target and for you?

Figure out the numbers on your own and then write it down in your AREA journal. Reading the tables is a good test of how well your target communicates. If you're looking at a chart that shows a correlation between two things, consider whether the correlation is meaningful or not.

For example, the following chart shows a very high correlation between per capita cheese consumption and the number of people who died by becoming tangled in their bedsheets, but logically we know that this is spurious. We tend to assume that data is accurate and meaningful, but it isn't always. As you conduct your research, remember not to eat too much cheese in bed, and to question all data.

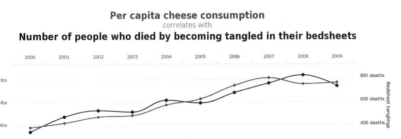

Courtesy of Tyler Virgen

There are many ways that data may be flawed. We'll touch on this again in the Analysis chapter, but for now, consider this point when reviewing data sets: always make sure you understand how a study was designed and conducted.

As Micah began the AREA research on his two university options, he knew that Hopkins was a top school with a national reputation. He was leaning heavily toward accepting Hopkins over Pitt based on that national reputation. But he decided that this was not a decision to make lightly, or upon social proof, in which we make decisions based upon what others think. With tens of thousands of dollars and Micah's future at stake, his parents felt this decision needed a rigorous and methodical process.

Micah started to gather numerical data about the colleges from his Absolute targets: the colleges themselves. He saw that Johns Hopkins' fact book advertised that its education, public health, and biomedical engineering programs were ranked number 1, according to *U.S. News & World Report*. Pitt's fact book didn't list its ranking.

In his Relative research, Micah knew he would want to look at *U.S. News & World Report* for both schools to see how they were ranked. But he stopped himself from concluding that Hopkins was "better" than the University of Pittsburgh because of this disclosure. Micah knew he needed to question the data specifically to determine how the rankings were compiled.

Moreover, Micah was surprised to learn that Johns Hopkins reported that only 20 percent of freshman with a declared interest in the pre-med program ultimately applied to medical school. However, it was encouraging to learn that of those students, more than 80 percent secured an acceptance to at least one medical school. He knew in Relative and Exploration research he would want to find out Pitt's numbers as they were not available on Pitt's website.

Furthermore, just by looking at the two schools' fact books, Micah noticed that they recorded very different numbers. Hopkins selected information that advertised its success, listing "firsts" such as inventing the first implantable rechargeable pacemaker in 1972, and the number of Nobel prizes the faculty at the university has received. In contrast, Pitt's fact book numbers told Micah what was happening currently at Pitt. It had a wealth of disclosure about the amount of research dollars that each part of the school received as well as a list of where the sponsored donations were coming from. Micah saw that the schools were focused on disclosing very different data and telling different stories. He liked the idea of being at a school like Hopkins with its august history, but Pitt showcased campus life and it looked intriguing.

Like Micah, John also had a gut reaction about his decision that he wanted to hold in check. He thought he should open a second clinic in Nepal because his first clinic was successful and he felt confident that he could replicate that success. However, he knew that he was making a big assumption and wanted to be more professional and mindful in order to have conviction in his decision. He didn't want to fall prey to the Planning Fallacy, which is our tendency to underestimate time, cost, and risks of completing a project. He also knew that he needed some research and data to present to potential funders so that they would support his expansion.

So what numbers did John research to begin his Absolute work about Oda's growth options? At first, John was concerned that there wouldn't be numbers. He quickly realized he was making another assumption because when he sat down to begin his work, he found some relevant facts and figures provided by his Absolute target, the Nepalese government.

He searched for information to better understand how Nepal sees and represents its healthcare system, and how the system works. He wanted to know how many healthcare facilities existed. What kind of facilities were they (clinic or hospital)? Where were they located? What kinds of medical services did they provide? What kinds of maladies were the most widespread and were the facilities able to adequately meet those needs?

He then checked this data against information he found about the area in which he was considering opening a clinic, along a major roadway. What other hospitals or clinics were nearby? Were there staffing numbers for each? Was there data about the kinds of illnesses that they treated?

This part of the Absolute research revealed a few things. First, it gave John a map of care options across the country. Further, it revealed that there was a shortfall in health services in the region he was considering. The nearest hospital serving that area was almost four hours away by car. For most people, this would mean a 12-hour journey on foot.

He also confirmed that the illnesses Oda's current facility treated were statistically consistent with illness rates in other areas of Nepal, so he felt confident that his team could deliver appropriate and useful care in a new facility.

However, once he looked at population data for the country, he realized that he'd begun with yet another incorrect assumption: he'd assumed the vast majority of the district's population was in its capital city. Instead, the data revealed that only about 6 percent of the district's population lived in a city. The result? The population where he was considering opening up a roadside clinic was much greater than he'd initially thought. Oda would need more staff in the clinic, more supplies, and a bigger budget to service the area properly, but could also have a bigger impact on health outcomes.

As he began thinking about health outcomes, John realized he couldn't make assumptions about the healthcare needs of the community that would be served by a new clinic. By raising his awareness about earlier assumptions, he recognized and avoided the salience bias. He would not assume that the health needs of a new community would exactly mirror Oda's existing clinic community. Yes, there was overlap, but what other services might Oda need to provide?

Many more answers and new questions came to light as well. The data John gathered from Nepal's government was old and incomplete in areas. John knew he would have to reconfirm or update some of the estimates in his "R" (Relative) phase of his AREA research to double check whether what he discovered here in Absolute was reliable.

Here is an example of John's Absolute research from his AREA journal.

- Option 1: Road facility single location
- AREA Absolute: Getting to Know Your Target

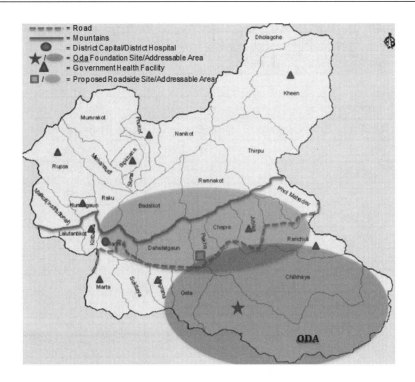

John found this map on Nepal's government website, which displays the geographic layout of the Kalikot District. He added his "coordinates" to the map. He drew a star where the Oda clinic is located and a square at the proposed location of the roadside clinic. Then he shaded in the catchment areas for each clinic. If Oda were to open a second clinic, it would need to be on the same southern side of the mountain where his existing clinic is located.

John found the following population data from his Absolute target, the Nepalese government, on its website for the Kalikot District. It indicated the population density of each Village Development Community (VDC) so that he could see how many people lived by each facility.

Population With Roadside Access		
VDC	Population	Percent of District
Institutional	431	0.23%
Jubitha	3,279	1.72%
Ranchuli	3,334	1.75%
Mugraha	3,925	2.05%
Phoi Mahadev	4,818	2.52%
Chhapre	5,089	2.66%
Odanaku	5,223	2.73%
Kotbada	5,435	2.85%
Gela	5,513	2.89%
Pakha	5,899	3.09%
Chilkhaya	6,451	3.38%
Sukataya	7,095	3.71%
Dahafatgaun	7,084	3.71%
Lalu	8,265	4.33%
Marta	9,958	5.21%
Manma	12,884	6.75%
Total	**94,684**	**49.57%**

Gela, Pakha, and Chilkhaya are the three catchment areas currently served by Oda. He identified Manma, Marta, and Dahafatgaun as part of the catchment for a new second clinic. He was excited to find this specific data, but he wasn't sure the data was reliable. He also missed its import: the larger population that a new clinic might service could turn out to be too many patients for Oda to handle.

Like John, you may collect data from your target that you don't fully understand. Or the data the data itself may be unreliable.

Given the influence of authority bias, it can be easy to take data as gospel, but don't. For example, the government collects inflation statistics. We all think of the government as a reliable, unbiased reporter. But the government uses those statistics to calculate increases in entitlement payments so it has an incentive to keep a lid on these numbers. Might your target have an incentive to show a result that might make its information unreliable?

For Bill, his Absolute work looked quite different from John's, but again he began with the numbers. He started by limiting his search to continuing care facilities within 10 miles of his parents' current home, identifying seven possible targets. He ruled out senior living options that didn't have a continuum of care, as his ideal goal was that his parents would age and stay in one place as their conditions and medical needs changed.

Next, he wanted to explore the costs of the different facilities. He was surprised to learn that very little actual cost information was available through the facilities' websites. Only one of the seven locations posted information. (The buy-in fee ranged from $119,000 for a single person to more than a million dollars for a 2-bedroom unit. There would be a monthly fee on top of the buy-in amount.) Was this expensive or average? He found no basis for comparison. Bill made a note that when he contacted facilities in the Exploration phase, he would get cost information and statistics about what percentage of residents lived in each part of the facility (independent living, assisted living, and memory care).

When Claudia looked at the tuition numbers for nursing programs and coding schools, she also had a bit of sticker shock. An accelerated RN degree might easily run her $40,000. Coding programs required a much smaller upfront investment. Still, she didn't want to choose a new career by upfront costs alone. She was looking at the long game. So although she started with the numbers, Claudia didn't stop there.

Your Target's Website

Once you've explored the numbers, it's time to look more broadly at the entity or entities you've identified as important (your Absolute target), and to dive into the website. The website is where your target makes its most public case and has the most latitude to describe what it does, why it does it, and how well it's succeeding.

Websites are flexible. They're not regulated, so they are valuable real estate in which the target can choose what it wants to say about itself with limited outside interference. Different entities will prioritize different information, but almost all will try to convey their value and their message to their target audience. Your goal here is to scour your target's website for data related to your decision. As you peruse the site, use the questions in Cheetah Sheet #3 as a template for the questions you will want to ask.

Cheetah Sheet 3: The Story of Your Target's Website

1. Who is the website targeting? How do you know?
   a. What does the target's homepage convey?
   b. How is the website set up and oriented? What tabs does it have?

2. What kind of content and language does the entity use on its site? Is it updated frequently?

3. What does the target advertise as its key accomplishments?

4. How does your target communicate its value? How does it back up that message? Is it relevant to you?

5. What is the narrative that the website tells?

6. Read how your target describes its numerical data, charts, and tables and consider whether that matches with how you understand its numerical data. Is there any discrepancy?

7. Is there important information missing or not available? (This is how an Absolute target shapes its story. For example, the facilities Bill investigated didn't include pricing data. This made him wonder about the organizations' lack of transparency.)

8. If the entity is a public company, how is the investor relations page set up? Is it easy to navigate and are the SEC filing links provided? How difficult is it to get financial and other business/operational information on the site?

The right questions will vary, but the goal here is to understand how your Absolute target sees itself, and to identify areas in which you might want to question the target's story. Write down the answers to these questions in your AREA journal.

Bill's Absolute research into the numbers was frustrating and unproductive. He had to step back from the emotional response to explore the targets' websites without judgment. He wanted to see what they had to say about themselves and not hold it against them that they hadn't been forthcoming with important financial information.

Claudia began by looking at the school websites for both careers as well as the websites of some of the major employers in both fields. This basic website search yielded a treasure trove of information for her, although not all of it was positive. Claudia heard that with the BA in Psychology she'd earned more than a decade ago, she could apply to accelerated R.N. degree programs, and could become a licensed R.N. in 18 months or less. This was much faster than the customary four-year degree program that a first-time college student would attend. Coding programs had an even faster timeline: she could be trained and working in the field in six months. But when she began researching, she discovered that neither career change option was as easy or straightforward as she had been led to believe.

Claudia's website searches revealed that both options had some unanticipated roadblocks. There were science course prerequisites for the nursing programs that she'd have to complete before applying. And the best coding schools also required up to 150 hours of pre-work.

As Micah began researching the two universities' websites, he had an interesting experience. He wanted to share what he'd seen with his parents, but when they gathered around the computer, the landing pages were different than they appeared from Micah's laptop computer. Micah recognized that these website visits were snapshots. He knew that websites continually update, but he was surprised at how different the homepage visuals were.

As you are visiting and re-visiting your target's website, be aware that your previous searches may color what you see. For example, when Micah looked at the Johns Hopkins website from his laptop, he got a different landing page than his family, even though they both visited the same URL and used the same web browser. As you are collecting information about an entity through its website, your browser is collecting information about you.

Although their landing pages were different, both Micah and his parents saw that the Hopkins website was clearly focused on the school's illustrious history. On his parents' landing page, Hopkins advertised itself as "America's first research university." The screen scrolled through a series of photos of an attractive campus, pulling the viewer in. However, there was no information about the university as it exists today. Even when they went to the "About Us" page, the school's focus was on its history. Hopkins was positioning itself to appeal to students who would want to be a part of this exciting history.

The University of Pittsburgh's landing page had less production value and was busier and more work-a-day, featuring recent happenings at the university, such as the football team's win over Syracuse. However, right in the center of the homepage was a box about "enrollment appointments" and an information bar for prospective students. The "About Us" page featured a video of undergraduates with the tag line "Pitt's history of building better lives." Along the right side of the page was a box that overviewed some of the important school statistics, such as the number of undergraduates, number of full- and part-time faculty, and the student-faculty ratio. Hopkins's website didn't provide that data. The Pitt website seemed to reach outward to a potential student body. Although Hopkins's website was focused on the impressive achievements of an august institution, Pitt's foregrounded students' potential future achievements.

Reading and analyzing the way your research target chooses to present itself gives you insight into its focus and, therefore, into how it thinks about its business.

As Bill reviewed the websites of the facilities for his parents, his initial Absolute goal was to find out and understand the basics: who, what, where, why, how, and when. He was interested in the level of independence that was available at each location, as well as medical and recreational services. Bill studied each option's floor plans and the resident make-up. He also wanted to evaluate whether the facilities looked new or were in need of repair. He was quickly able to rule out three of the seven locations, as they did not offer a true independent living option.

Exploring the websites of his four remaining targets, Bill realized that 10 miles might sound close, but in Westchester it was an enormous distance because of how the county is shaped. Bill had poorly framed a Critical Concept since it was important for his parents to maintain their established physician relationships; keeping them close was non-negotiable.

Two of the facilities Bill targeted had great onsite medical services, but their physicians were affiliated with community hospitals on the other side of the county from where Bill's parents currently lived. They were a no-go.

After a relatively quick website review, Bill refined his Critical Concepts and narrowed his choices down to two facilities: The Osborne in Rye and Westchester Meadows in Valhalla. Both offered a variety of floor plans, and both offered a true range of care, from independent living and assisted living to hospice and memory care. Bill was also pleased that The Osborne was affiliated with the medical group his parents already used.

Bill's Absolute work raised more questions than it answered, but it helped him nail his Critical Concepts and hone in on what was important.

As he moved into his Relative phase of research, Bill wanted to address that he'd been unable to get basic pricing information from his two research targets, and knew that this would continue to be a major concern. However, he also wanted to learn about the two facilities from other perspectives. Specifically, he wanted to know if the residents were happy there, investigate any complaints, and read reviews of the places. By doing a thorough job on his Absolute research, Bill felt he gained a good understanding of how the facilities saw themselves and wanted to be seen. He had a list of questions and felt prepared to move on to Relative research.

Your Target's Press Releases

Beyond the website, your Absolute target also communicates officially through press releases. What does it talk about when it issues communication?

Cheetah Sheet 4: Your Target's Official Statements

1. How does your Absolute target use its power to release information? Is the information specific and material or promotional and speculative? This gets at content and motivation.

2. How often does the target issue press releases? Frequency conveys not only how often the target wants to communicate or how self-promotional it is, but also gives critical information about what news its leaders consider to be important.

3. Look at the tone and word choice of the releases. What do they convey?

4. Are press releases for only major announcements or for small and seemingly marginal news as well? Is there evidence to back up assertions in the releases?

Claudia found that NYU's College of Nursing included a press release applauding a faculty member for an editorial that waded into a debate about whether nurses should be able to take the place of doctors as primary care physicians. She wondered whether this impacted the reputation of the school among hospitals and employers. Would it be harder for her to get a placement if she came out of a program that was known for being controversial? It was another data point in what she was learning about NYU's nursing program. In her website search, Claudia noted that NYU's tuition was the highest of all of the nursing programs she was investigating, and their rules on transferring credits seemed tough. She knew she'd want to research more about these concerns in her AREA Relative and Exploration research.

Your Target's Leadership

Next consider reading about leadership/management. Some decision-makers will want to learn about their entity's key people, the "who" of your Absolute target, including their qualifications, decisions, and impact. The specifics will vary for each situation; not all high-stakes decisions need a leadership investigation.

For John, it was critical. All of his options had an element of government dependency. An inept leader could hurt his organization's reputation, or the promises that the government made to him. If he opted to open a second clinic, the government promised to donate a building to house this new roadside facility. If he opted to partner with the government, John would be working directly within the government's health network. If he opted to invest in drones, he would likely need the government's okay, and perhaps assistance, to facilitate the drone shipments and medical supply dissemination.

So the next step to understanding John's opportunities was exploring the government's healthcare office, figuring out how it ran, and who was in charge. What kinds of accomplishments and record did the office and leaders have? What might John learn about the office and characters from letting the records speak for themselves? "People were walking for hours each day to get to our clinic," said John. "They said they couldn't get care anywhere else. But was that based upon a lack of facilities, or a question about the quality of the government's healthcare, or both?"

For Bill, the individual members of the continuing care facilities' boards might not matter, but he did want to know who ran them. Were the leaders new? What kind of background did they have? Were they long-term healthcare professionals, or did they have a hospitality industry background? What might the bios reveal about the focus of the leader?

For Claudia deciding between nursing and computer programming, issues like job placement, cost and length of training, and income potential were more critical than investigating who ran a particular coding school or nursing program. Program leadership was a 12th or 13th Critical Concept; not one she really needed to focus on, although she had taken notes on the controversial NYU press release.

In exploring Hopkins and Pitt, Micah didn't get lost in the whole universities, but stayed focused on the pre-med programs. He didn't need to consider who the university presidents were, but he did want to identify the main players in the pre-med programs. Who were the advisors? Who were the key professors? Who was doing interesting medical research? By getting to know the names of the key players, he set himself up for the next phase of his AREA research.

For both schools, Micah looked at course listings and identified the names of the professors in chemistry, physics, and organic chemistry. He set this information aside, knowing he'd search both College Confidential and RateMyProfessor.com in Relative research.

Cheetah Sheet 5: Learning About the Leadership

1. What kind of a leader does the target have? A hands-on manager or more of a strategic leader? A salesman or an engineer? Is she promotional or cautious?

2. How did she arrive in the top spot and what might that say about her strengths and weaknesses?

3. What are her key accomplishments prior to, and in, this position? What has the impact of those accomplishments been on the target?

4. What is her compensation and how is it structured? What incentives does she have to perform and over what period of time? If you are looking at a publicly traded company, the proxy statement contains this information. If you are looking at a charity, check out its Form 990.

One type of leader or chief executive is not necessarily better than another. But it is important to identify a leader's strengths and weaknesses and think about how well or poorly her interests align with the target's goals. It can also be important to know how a leader came into her role, whether she has been with the entity for a long time or whether she was recruited from the outside and what her previous experience has been. In a similar vein, learning about what the leader perceives as her key accomplishments may give you insight into what she values. Have those successes paid off for the organization? Many an organization has been saved by a dynamic leader or sunk by the wrong fit.

In addition, you can learn a lot by understanding how the leader is compensated. How is she economically motivated? Some leaders or CEOs have a lot of money tied up in the entity's long-term future prospects through deferred compensation or options packages. Some are paid mostly in cash. These compensation structures result in different incentives that can play out in unexpected ways.

Your Target's Research Reports

To finish off the basics from the Absolute perspective, I recommend searching to see if your target has published any research, policy reports, or proposals on an issue. John looked at whether Nepal's government had put out any statements that showed a healthcare focus or initiative that might complement or conflict with Oda's core competencies.

When Bill looked to see whether the continuing care facilities had published position papers, he stumbled across The Osborne's policy discussion, which disclosed that it used residents' protected health information for research purposes. Was that standard? Were the residents informed of this policy? He wasn't sure what to make of that, but might that research benefit the residents? Could it mean his parents might get cutting-edge medical care or could it mean they'd get unnecessary testing? He'd want to find out in his AREA Exploration research.

Cheetah Sheet 6: Your Target's Position Papers

1. What does your target take a position on and why?

2. What positions does it take?

3. If it's a research paper, are the research partners credible? Where did the funding for the study come from?

4. Why has the target divulged this information? What is the incentive to put out the paper? Is there a way to determine its impact?

AREA Thesis Statements

Take a Cheetah Pause and craft a clear, concise, and cogent thesis statement that summarizes your conclusions from the Absolute phase of research. The statement should answer questions such as "What have I learned here and what is the implication of that knowledge?" or "What is the meaning of my target's story in its own words?" This step puts together the five parts of your Absolute research, or as many as you've deemed useful (for example, your target's numbers, website, official statements, leadership team's perspective, and research reports).

It's difficult to write a good thesis statement. However, I believe it is critically important to do, and when done well, it can provide you with "aha moments." A compelling thesis statement is an upfront time investment that will save you time later on. By forcing you to reach conclusions about discrete sections of research, you are not just collecting information, but also synthesizing and analyzing your work as you progress. Focusing on the significance of the information hones your Critical Concepts so that you refine them, making your research process continually more effective and efficient on specifically what matters to *you*.

Writing *is* thinking. Having to write the thesis out—putting your work and its significance into the language of a cause and effect—often points out the holes in your understanding. As Albert Einstein said, "If you can't explain it simply, you don't understand it well enough." I find this true time and again; when I am struggling to make a clear argument (when I can't define what I've done or why) it usually means I need to do more work.

A good thesis statement represents three things: your research, your findings, *and* your interpretation. This last point, the interpretation, is critical. It means that you've taken the time not only to conduct research, but also to figure out the "So what?" What does it all mean? It asks you to chunk your learning because it asks you to be specific, expresses a main idea, *and* to take a stand.

At its best, a clear, concise, and cogent thesis statement will consist of just a few sentences that can be supported and explained by means of examples and evidence. Here is an example of a thesis written by an Associated Press reporter after Abraham Lincoln was shot in Ford's Theatre in 1865. Although this is the lede of a news article, in its brevity and clarity it illustrates some of the best components of a thesis:

> *The President was shot in a theatre tonight and perhaps mortally wounded.*

In this example, the first half of the thesis statement demonstrates that its author has gathered and compiled evidence. The second half of the thesis statement shows the analysis of that evidence leading to an insight. Note that the news lead is clear, concise, and cogent. It makes an argument for what *will happen* based upon all the evidence present at the time. It gives the reader the news *and* its implication. Of course, "perhaps mortally wounded" is a judgment call, and is based upon the perspective of the reporter's sources. All thesis statements make a judgment call and that call is only as good as the data that informs it.

Your thesis statements should answer the following questions: What is the information you've collected? What perspective does it come from? What does it all mean? Based upon what you know at this point, what is your judgment call?

Recording your evidence, thoughts, and convictions in a thesis statement can point you to what you need to research next, or point out gaps in your work that need to be addressed before moving forward. Consider what your thesis statement at each point is directing you to investigate next. Follow the signposts. They can teach you many things about not only the decisions that work out well, but also those that won't turn out as planned.

By the end of the AREA process, you will have a series of thesis statements to compare, contrast, and knit together. With a concrete record of your thinking, you won't have to recreate your ideas and won't easily fall prey to hindsight bias, where we fool ourselves into thinking something that might not have been so.

As you have further questions that come out of each thesis statement you develop, I suggest that you write down every question that arises from the research process, and answer the questions as you go along. Never erase the questions so that you retain the trail of your thinking as you map out your AREA of investigation.

Being a good researcher is not only about the quality of your decisions but also about the results that come from those decisions.

Your research may not be efficient at this stage, and that's fine. These tips help you become effective so that the time and attention now will accelerate your work later on. The goal is to streamline your decision-making by bringing structure and focus to the process.

Here are the three Absolute thesis statements John wrote so that you can see them together:

Roadside Clinic: While a private roadside clinic would be a new healthcare delivery system in Kalikot, Nepal, there is a clear and present need for such a facility. It would more than double our potential patient visits to more than 20,000 annually, would add three staff members, and about $24,000 of expenses to our annual budget, necessitating an increase of about $36,000 in fundraising, of which approximately $20,000 would need to be identified.

Government Partnership: Working with the government's health clinics would allow us to leverage a strong government relationship and existing health infrastructure to engage new communities, provide a wider dispersal of basic medical care, and conduct a comprehensive district-wide needs analysis. The most recent census data validates this, indicating more than 95,000 people and greater than 50% of the district lives more than four hours from a road. This option would add one staff member and have a $29,000 budget, of which about $19,000 would need to be identified.

Drone Medical Kit Delivery: Drone technology has not played a significant role in the development sector in Nepal, but this technology is being explored in developing countries and has the potential for an array of medical applications. Given the distances and altitudes specified by Oda's pilot program, along with limited cultural and regulatory barriers, the technology has economic and operational feasibility. However, with more than 250 companies in approximately

60 countries producing drones, prices ranging from $500 to hundreds of thousands of dollars, funding and operating partnerships would be needed, as well as much more research to learn about the industry and logistics.

These thesis statements sum up a lot of research. By pausing to answer "So what?" John's thesis statements achieve several things in only a few sentences. They take into account the issue he is exploring, his understanding of its implications in terms of both a needs assessment and an economic assessment, and his determination that the options are viable.

"The Absolute research showed me that I didn't need to rule out any of my options yet and it gave me a clear idea of what I needed to do next. I'd never done much research before and certainly never followed such a structured, methodical process," he said. "By narrowing my lens to think just about primary information from my target, I had to think creatively. I was collecting information in an organized way, but categorizing it by its source was invaluable. It not only showed me the government's viewpoint but kept me distant from my own. I studied what the government claims to do, how it does it, and where its facilities are located."

The research and thesis achieved their goals by enabling John to move on with a concise summary of his work to date and to provide him with a clear signpost for future research. A Critical Concept would be to understand the reputation of the government. Did it honor its promises? Did people trust its services? If he chose to partner with the government, he would want to know that the clinics didn't sit empty because their association with the government meant they automatically had a poor reputation for care.

"After my Absolute work, I realized I had five Critical Concepts," said John. "I needed to understand whether each option had government support as well as community support. I needed to know what costs were involved, and what impact the option would have on healthcare in our Kalikot region. And I needed to figure out whether each option fit with our core competencies."

At times, you may find that your narratives conflict, or tell different stories. At this point, it is important to *pause.*

Cheetah Sheet 7: A Final Look

1. Why might the target of your research tell its story differently in different arenas, for example, their website versus a press release?

2. What incentives might it have to represent itself in different ways to different audiences?

3. Where can you look to investigate the discrepancies that you've identified?

The answers to all of these questions will come in the rest of your AREA research, specifically in Relative and Exploration. As you work through your Absolute research, you may be tempted to jump the gun and start looking at other, secondary sources. Don't! By doing the Absolute research first, and thoroughly, you keep your perspectives separate, which will better enable you to assess them dispassionately. And by spending time to complete a thoughtful Absolute investigation, you are unearthing the entire foundation of your decision. Your future research will help you determine if that foundation is solid or porous. But until you've unearthed the entire foundation, you can't begin to judge its quality.

3

AREA = R: Relative

> Don't waste life in doubts and fears; spend yourself
> on the work before you, well assured that the right
> performance of this hour's duties will be the best
> preparation for the hours and ages that will follow it.
>
> —Ralph Waldo Emerson

There's a wonderful passage in the classic children's book *Alice in Wonderland* that exemplifies the importance of a focused decision-making process. Young Alice approaches the Cheshire Cat and asks, "Would you tell me, please, which way I ought to go from here?"

"That depends a good deal on where you want to get to," said the Cat.

"I don't much care where," said Alice.

"Then it doesn't matter which way you go," said the Cat.

"So long as I get somewhere," Alice added as an explanation.

"Oh, you're sure to do that," said the Cat, "if only you walk long enough."

In making high-stakes decisions, there are so many potential sources of information and options for analysis that it is imperative to keep in mind "where you want to get to." Needless to say, time management is a critical component of doing the job well.

The goal of the AREA Method is to make steady, well-informed progress toward evaluating your options to arrive at the best decision for you. The method helps you manage your research process by directing how and where to conduct research strategically. It then suggests Cheetah Pauses—the strategic stops that guide you to "chunk" your learning, assessing discrete pieces of data within a perspective, and summing up by crafting a narrative summary thesis at set points.

Since most research is not linear, to recognize and uncover an important observation you need to *pause* and think to reorient yourself in pursuit of your Critical Concepts. Perhaps a previously glossed-over data point has gained critical importance or perhaps a previously planned course of research has been rendered unproductive.

In the Relative phase of AREA, you will use the theses you developed in the Absolute phase to build upon the information you've collected and put it into a broader context. In other words, in Relative, you take a different perspective. Relative sources are sources that are somehow connected (related) to your research target, but are not from the target itself.

John came away from Absolute unsure about the reliability of the government's data and healthcare system. In Relative, he wanted to take a different perspective on the Nepalese government and he wanted to explore the perspectives of other nonprofits that operated in developing countries with problematic governments. He was particularly interested in organizations that had worked in emergency situations comparable to Nepal's post-earthquake landscape.

His Relative sources included other health organizations, watchdog groups, and both non-profit and for-profit entities working in Nepal, suppliers to these organizations, and the people who use them. For John, and for you, these external sources offer a filtered view of the research target as well as opinions and facts that will color your perception of the target's story and your Critical Concepts.

The Relative phase will serve to vet and supplement the Absolute phase, expanding and either confirming information you have gleaned from the Absolute phase or exposing a disconnect between the information your Absolute target presents and the information that is presented from outside sources. Pay special attention to the debates or conflicts between different perspectives you encounter; these can guide your Critical Concepts and help you gain an edge.

The "R" category of research will follow different paths to solve different high-stakes problems. You may begin the "R" phase of research in the comfort of your own home with the Internet, but you may need the in-person help of a research librarian. Today's librarian won't walk you into musty, mildew-smelling stacks to locate an ancient tome about the War of 1812. Instead, he'll help you navigate little known or pricey databases with expert searches. He may even give you the library's access code for LexisNexis (a database of legal cases) or Medline (a database of medical journal articles), or work with you to create the most effective keyword searches of the National Newspaper Index.

For all AREA "R" work, there is an element of verification of AREA "A," as well as reinforcing and refining your Critical Concepts. The work as you enter this next concentric circle of data includes the following research tasks:

1. Mapping your Absolute target's ecosystem (that is, the actors and entities that play different roles in the target's environment) and a relevant competitive analysis.

2. Conducting a literature review to locate news articles and papers about the target or issue you are researching so you can see the target as it is interpreted by others.

As you explore these facets, you will come across many names of people who have information about your research target. They will include not only people quoted in news articles, including experts, academics, competitors, and customers, but also the reporters who wrote the stories. Compile a list of these potential sources in your AREA journal in order to later prepare for the Exploration phase of the AREA Method, where you will learn to conduct in-depth interviews.

Cheetah Sheet 8: Planning Ahead for Exploration

1. Record the names and contact information for each potential source.

2. Write down where you found the source's name and in what context.

3. Note how you think this person may help you understand what you've identified to be your Critical Concepts.

Once you've done this spadework for Exploration, it's time to turn your full attention to Relative. Begin with a business and industry map.

What did a map look like for John at Oda, for Bill researching his folks' living situation, for advertising executive Claudia and her career change, and for Micah choosing between Pitt and Johns Hopkins? Let's start with discussing the value of a general mapping exercise.

A business and industry analysis and map will put your research targets in context and help you identify important issues in evaluating their ecosystem. In many cases, the mapping exercise should not just look at your subset of options but your subset within the larger universe so you understand how your targets stack up against the best and the worst out there. In some cases (both Micah's and Claudia's, for example) mapping just your subset of options is the right way to go.

Although Bill's search had very quickly narrowed down to two continuing care locations, he wanted a map that pulled information from across the industry nationwide. It remained an option for Bill's parents to move to another house, one with a first-floor bedroom, instead of a continuing care facility, so Bill wanted to be sure that the facilities in Westchester compared favorably nationwide. He wanted to compare his very narrow options against a broader background. He used the *U.S. News & World Report* ranking of nursing homes and read about the top continuing care facilities to assess whether the features and care at his local choices matched some of the features that gave the top-ranked places their edge.

For Micah, however, an industry map of all pre-med programs or the best pre-med programs wasn't that useful because he had a complicated choice to make in a short period of time and it was an either/or choice. Therefore, Micah made an industry map of medical schools that accept students from Pitt and Johns Hopkins.

Claudia needed to develop two industry maps—one for nursing and one for computer programming. Like Micah, she was best served by mapping her selected programs against each other. It wasn't productive to look at the entire universe of either field. She wanted something local or something online and there were enough options that she could compare among them.

Her nursing industry map laid out the different nursing schools available to her. None of the programs were close to where she lived, but there was a range of options in and around New York City, as well as one very good program farther out on Long Island. She had hoped to consider online programs, but discovered that most of the accelerated B.S.N. programs online were for R.N.s seeking a bachelor's degree. However, she found one intriguing online possibility: Gwynedd Mercy University, located in Pennsylvania, which had a distance learning option for non-nurses and offered the pre-requisite courses she needed.

Her nursing industry map included the pre-reqs she thought she'd need to fill, the cost, length of time, pass rates for each program, and their job placement data. Claudia mapped teaching hospitals versus county or local hospitals, and whether or not the nurses were unionized. She also considered how the Affordable Care Act was impacting nurses' hours and wages. This gave her more information about the quality of her nursing choices.

Claudia made a similar map for computer programming and was relieved to discover that more of the coding schools were online. However, she found that the length of the programs, programming language focus, and job placement varied widely. It was a more confusing landscape. It seemed to assume a level of knowledge of the field that Claudia did not have.

The map exercise helped her to understand that the programming options were more specialized than the nursing option, for which everyone takes the same licensing exam. In programming, Claudia needed to know what she wanted to specialize in before she started, whereas nursing did not require that she knew the outcome before she would begin the training.

Your goal is to check up on what you've learned so far. What are your target's strengths and weaknesses? What is its position within the field and how do others portray it? Often conflicting information will exist about the quality of a target's operation. This stage of research will help you clarify the conflicts. For example, Micah worried that a Pitt education was not equivalent to a Johns Hopkins education. Mapping the medical schools that students from each institution were accepted into allowed him to see an apples-to-apples comparison.

John knew that Nepal lacked a sophisticated and modern healthcare system, but what were the implications of the system's weaknesses for Oda's success?

The map can better educate you about your target's core competencies and how it achieves its objectives. In making her maps, Claudia discovered that nursing schools were both transparent and remarkably similar in their course loads because of the licensing exam that all students must take. The coding schools were more of a black box. It was harder to compare them. The coding school map was more confusing because there were so many options, both in the end-result skill set and the paths to get there.

The map should provide you with an assessment of what your target offers (products and services), when it offers it (timing, business cycles, and so on), where the entity makes those offers (markets and segments), and at what price (its competitive plan). For example, Bill's map would help him understand what services each continuing care facility offered, whether there were age or capability limitations on their resident population, what part of the elderly market they served, and the costs for those services.

You want to put your target in context because it is not only shaped by its actions, but by the environment around it. Think of a good athlete on a bad team: by placing your target in a map, you can see the whole team. John was concerned that even if Oda could provide quality healthcare, by delivering it through government health clinics with a poor reputation, Oda's impact might be blunted or its reputation tainted.

John's map included other international healthcare and aid organizations that operated in Nepal, but also a few that did similar work in mobile care walk-in clinics in other developing countries with struggling healthcare systems. He wanted to understand how the organizations in Nepal interacted with the government system and what their experiences had been. Then he replicated that research to understand how the other healthcare-related non-profits handled similar struggles. He looked at information from USAID, the Red Cross, the World Health Organization, and more. He noted that these organizations focused on preventative care, while the healthcare infrastructure in Nepal consisted primarily of hospitals equipped for treatment.

In addition to seeing whether these organizations' data about Nepal's facilities and care matched the government's data, John was also interested in what kinds of patient problems these organizations identified as prevalent. John had learned in his Absolute research that the most common ailments among the Nepalese in his region were digestive system problems, fever of unknown origin, fractures, and trauma. Information from the WHO corroborated the government's data he had collected in Absolute. These were all issues that Oda was well equipped to handle.

Yet John's Relative research also uncovered that Nepal suffered from a staffing problem in remote areas. John said there were reports of "the healthcare team moving on, while the patient remains. Not only was there a lot of turnover, but also a lot of absenteeism." This was a big discovery: if the government system was not reliable, would linking Oda's services with the government's tarnish his organization's reputation, especially if patients could not distinguish between his employees and the government's?

All of these mapping exercises are meant to set your research target in context and prepare you for the kinds of questions you will ask in your Literature Review. Once you've completed your business/industry map, take a Cheetah Pause and write out a thesis statement for your map's narrative. Record it in your AREA journal and compare it to what you learned about your target in the Absolute phase of your research.

John's industry map showed that there were 30 health clinics run by the government and that they were not uniform. They varied in size, scope, and reputation. John knew that Oda would not be able to spread itself across all 30 clinics, but based on what he learned through his industry map, he believed that Oda could still partner with the government to work with some of the clinics. He crafted a thesis statement for his government partnership option that read as follows:

Globally, mobile health clinics have proven effective in reaching isolated populations when augmented by a stable primary health care strategy. The main constraint affecting mobile clinics is the temporary nature of the care dispensed, in other words "what to do when the mobile team moves on, and the patient remains." To diminish this issue, planned efforts should explore how big the problem is in Nepal and potentially drift toward health promotion and preventative activities in addition to a district-wide needs analysis.

This thesis provided essential information about two of John's CCs for working with the government's clinics. First, it addressed whether mobile health units were considered effective (they were) and then whether they were effective in Nepal (they were not consistently effective). It also got at a third CC: understanding the government's reputation among the population for dispensing quality healthcare (inconsistent).

And though the Absolute thesis for the government partnership option posited that Nepal's healthcare system would allow Oda to leverage a strong government relationship and existing healthcare infrastructure to engage new communities and provide a wider dispersal of basic medical care, his AREA "R" map complicated this notion. It undercut the Absolute finding and provided a signpost for John to investigate linking up with the government clinics in a different and more arms-length way so that Oda maintained its independence from the government's poor record. The thesis gave him a clear direction for where to do more research.

Literature Review

Once you've completed your industry map, the next step is to conduct a literature review. A literature review is a study of the published material about a particular subject. It is valuable because it gives you a wider lens on your research target and enables you to not only gather new information but also to put older information in context.

Cheetah Sheet 9: Literature Review

1. What does the broader world think about your targets in published articles and news stories?

2. What is the article's main idea or purpose?

3. What action is the writer advocating? Why? Does it make sense?

4. Are specific sources in the broader world credible?

5. Where has the article been published?

6. Who wrote the article?

7. What kind of publication did it appear in?

8. What seems to be the writer's incentive and how can you tell?

9. Do you find evidence of bias? Is there more than one view presented?

A literature review helps you understand how the outside world perceives your target and what issues other participants are focused on. Understanding what others are focused on can guide you to the key debates or issues impacting your decision. For example, when Claudia conducted her Absolute review for coding schools, she noticed that different schools reported different job placement data. Some schools only reported placement data anecdotally, while others had great placement numbers available right on their website. She'd made a note about exploring this topic in Relative.

When she began her Relative review, Claudia came across several blog posts and online articles that questioned the great outcome the schools had trumpeted. Many of the posts urged caution as the number of schools was growing rapidly and no accreditation system yet existed. The posts highlighted that job placement data was both fuzzy and changing very quickly; of the great placement numbers that had been trumpeted by some schools, another blog post noted that some stats included non-coding placements. One website devoted to promoting coding schools conducted a study that examined 44 coding programs to look at job placement and salaries. It showed that not only was the average starting salary falling, but the number of days it took graduates to find full-time employment had increased substantively from 2014 to 2015.

The more Claudia read, the more confusing the picture became. Although she knew that blog posts are often more opinion pieces than general news articles and aren't necessarily fact-checked, Claudia recognized that she needed a deeper dive and would definitely need to speak to people in the field. Her literature review pointed out a red flag that she'd want to research in Exploration. She made a list of questions generated from the stories along with a list of sources that included reporters, bloggers, and experts in the field. She wrote these names in her AREA journal.

The literature review summary not only enables you to recap the important information from the source, it also forces you to synthesize the information. It might open up new interpretations of old material, combine new material with old interpretations, or trace the intellectual progression of your target's field, including major debates. For Claudia it did all of these things. Your goal is to uncover the target's story as it is understood by the media and industry experts and then *pause* and evaluate.

Cheetah Sheet 10: What's the Story?

1. What is the thesis statement/narrative from the literature review? How does the emerging story explain why and how your research target does what it does?

2. Does your target lose its Absolute narrative in the literature review part of the Relative phase? In other words, are there better storytellers about your target? Consider where the storytelling power resides. Is it with the target or with some other source and why?

3. What are the source's biases/incentives? How are they reflected in the stories they tell and how should that color your interpretation of their stories?

4. Does the information present similar/different problems for your research target? Is there a consensus? Why? Do you think it is valid based upon your Absolute work?

5. Do the sources have evidence to back their claims? Do the opinions, facts, or anecdotes seem credible? How can you tell?

6. Does your literature review agree or disagree with your thesis statement from the Absolute phase? Why? To what degree? How does the media perception of your target differ from how your target presents itself?

7. How does any disagreement impact your understanding of your Critical Concepts and potential decision?

The first place most of us would start is with an Internet search, but after that search, consider other resources to investigate your target more thoroughly, such as setting up Google alerts or filters for your target and competitors. Now is also the time to get out your library card.

You can also search government websites for reports and statistics. Legal databases such as LexisNexis, Westlaw, and Pacer, which enable you to search legal cases in the federal appellate courts as well as district and bankruptcy courts, are useful. In addition, industry trade organizations, conferences, and publications can be good places to see what topics the target's industry is discussing, assess who is asked to speak at industry conferences, and which companies they work for to understand leaders in the field. Consider:

- Academic journals.
- Background-check websites like Accurint.com that collect public records and help detect fraud, verify identities, and more.
- Research-sharing websites like Gartner Group or Consumer Reports.
- Online complaint sites such as the Ripoff Report and the Better Business Bureau.
- Sources for industry history such as Wikipedia and annual reports.

It's also worth looking for articles and research insights about the broader *topic* at hand, beyond the target itself. When you complete your literature review, take a Cheetah Pause and construct one or more thesis statements from your Relative work phase.

Bill's initial Google search for Westchester Meadows turned up a *New York Times* article about the facility. He had resisted the urge to read the article during his Absolute research, but in Relative, he began with it. Although the article was a few years old, it contained the first pricing information that Bill found. There was a range of costs, but residents were paying at least $250,000 upfront in a bond that would be returned either to them if they left or to their heirs upon death. Additionally, residents were required to take out a long-term care policy for $23,000 (which they would not get back), and then pay between $2,500 and $4,500 monthly for their care. One of the residents interviewed noted that "It's not cheap, but it's high quality." That was what Bill and his parents were looking for: high quality.

Bill knew that he'd want to get more up-to-date pricing information in his Exploration phase. He wondered what services and care were included and what was a la carte. If his folks needed physical therapy, was that extra? He also wanted to understand what would happen to monthly costs as someone moved from independent living to assisted living. And was the move from independent living to assisted living easy, or were there waiting lists to move from one part of the facility to another?

Next, Bill looked at the *2015 U.S. News & World Report* ranking for nursing homes. Although his parents were not moving into the nursing home part of the facilities, the goal was that they could age in place there, moving from independent living to assisted living or even into a rehabilitation or memory care unit if needed. Bill learned that both Wetschester Meadows and the Osborn were highly rated as top nursing homes. Bill reviewed how the lists were compiled. They included many data points about patient care. For example, the rankings included the percentage of long-stay residents who had received the pneumococcal vaccine and how that compared to the national average. Both of Bill's targets ranked favorably when compared nationally.

Bill felt comfortable with the way the rankings had been determined. However, he did note that the rankings could not tell him anything about the experience of being a healthy senior living independently in one of these facilities.

These facts that Bill uncovered raised important questions about how the two facilities actually operated, questions that he knew he would want to explore in the Exploration phase of research. He and his parents would need to visit and observe the places, speak with the facilities staff, and, if possible, stay for lunch and chat with residents.

Before Bill moved into his Exploration research, he tried one more literature search; what he discovered threw a wrench into his plans. He narrowed his search terms to specify local coverage of the two facilities and he discovered an article from just a month prior that said Westchester Meadows might be filing for bankruptcy protection. Although he couldn't find any definitive information on whether the facility had yet filed, he wouldn't feel comfortable settling his parents into a place that might be financially unstable.

As Bill wrote out his thesis statement from his literature review, he realized that looking beyond just a mainstream news search really provided him with a crucial piece of information—one that he would have missed otherwise. The numerical data he found in Absolute, he also realized, had largely been supplied by the facilities themselves, as was the data used for the *U.S. News* rankings.

Although Bill checked how the *U.S. News* rankings were compiled, he didn't realize what was missing: The rankings included nothing about the financial wellbeing of the facilities. Bill realized that not only would he need to carefully and thoroughly investigate the Meadows in his Exploration phase, but he would also need to circle back into Absolute to increase the number of Absolute targets he researched, and to look at alternative housing and care options for his parents. It was time to look at a two-step move as well. What were the single-floor real estate options available? He also decided to revisit the Atria in Rye Brook, which was independent living only. He'd initially dismissed the Atria facility because it wasn't a continuing care facility, but the parent company had other sites that did offer continuing care in the Tri-State area. Would it be easier to move between facilities once you already lived in an Atria facility?

During his Absolute phase of research, Micah saw on the Johns Hopkins website that *U.S. News & World Report* ranked Hopkins as the 12th best university in the United States. Now, he went to the *U.S. News & World Report* site to learn where Pitt was located. It was ranked 62nd (in a six-way tie with five other universities). Sixty-two seemed much lower than 12. However, the list only included 199 rankings. Micah knew there were thousands of colleges and universities across the United States. So if both Hopkins and Pitt made it into the top half of the list, maybe that wasn't such a big difference.

He also checked the *U.S. News & World Report* rankings for the two schools' medical schools. Although *U.S. News* wasn't the only source of higher education rankings, it was widely perceived as a leading authority. He was aware of Hopkins' reputation before looking at its medical school and was not surprised to learn that Johns Hopkins Hospital was the number-one ranked hospital in its region. However, from his literature review, he learned that University of Pittsburgh's Medical Center was ranked number two in its region. The two medical schools were almost identical in their rankings in key areas of study such as pediatrics and women's health. This began to change Micah's thinking about Pitt. He realized he had not really known anything about the university's medical school and hospital. Now it changed the way he researched its impact on undergraduates and their experience at the school.

Micah also didn't blindly accept the rankings; he questioned the data. He searched for how the data was compiled and noticed that the magazine discloses that it changes its methodology from year to year. Further, the rankings were based in part on professor salaries, alumni giving, and the financial resources of the school, all potentially skewing data that may not be that relevant to the undergraduate experience.

In Absolute, Micah was concerned by the percentage of students who seemed to be dropping out of the pre-med program at Johns Hopkins and he wanted to know how that compared with Pitt's numbers, which he hadn't been able to find on Pitt's website. He'd also made a list of professors who taught the major required courses. In this phase of research, he read up on the key professors and tried to locate information about Pitt's pre-med completion rate.

Micah ran a search and noted that on RateMyProfessor.com, some of the Hopkins professors weren't rated at all, and the ones who were had only a few ratings but were rated poorly. In contrast, several of the professors at Pitt were rated quite highly, and the comments added important detail. About one chemistry professor, students said things like "[he] is absolutely fantastic. I've never met anyone who cares more about his students learning the material" and "I am not very good at chem, but [this professor] presented the material in a very clear way. He is also very charismatic!" Micah knew he'd want to speak to students at Hopkins about the professors to see whether the ratings accurately reflected students' experiences.

Like Micah, you may be unable to find information in your Absolute and Relative research that you expected. This doesn't mean you stop looking. It means you have to find the information at a different point, often through Exploration.

For Claudia, Relative information—newspaper articles about the exploding world of coding schools and news stories about the urgent need for more nurses—led her to think about a career change. What she discovered in this round of Relative research was that both nursing and coding were, by all accounts, growth fields. The perspective of her Absolute research seemed to be right in line with the perspective of her Relative research. However, her Relative research had raised a number of questions about the coding schools in particular. It was a growth field, but the growth was uneven and in some areas seemed to be slowing. Nursing, again, seemed more straightforward.

Claudia also learned that the nursing field would allow continued growth beyond the B.S.N. degree with jobs such as Nurse Practitioner, Certified Nurse midwife, and Nurse Anesthetist. Nursing was increasingly looking like the surer bet.

The goal here in Relative is to widen your lens as you pull back from your Absolute research target. You're setting your target into a broader context of its industry's or field's dynamics. The Relative research map feeds the questions you ask of your literature review, which will, in turn, feed the sources for your Exploration work. The sources will provide content, context, and color on your research that can't be easily understood from documents alone. To frame your work you want to check your CCs again. Have they changed or been amended? Are there new CCs worth adding? How does this new layer of information further enhance your research, and how may it be tainted by the sources of information?

For John, his literature review included examining other, more well-established non-profit health organizations operating in the developing world, including Partners in Health, which provides basic health services in Haiti, and Basic Health El Salvador, which focuses on women's issues. He heard about how Basic Health works with the government of El Salvador and receives logistical support, including busing patients from many miles away to get screening and treatments. Learning about these strategies helped John consider different ways that he might ask for support from Nepal's government.

One paper in particular that John came across was from the Red Cross discussing mobile health units. The paper included a Visual Map that laid out the Red Cross's definition of primary healthcare, which is displayed on page 101. John was surprised at the variety of activities that the Red Cross counted under the umbrella of "primary healthcare." They included providing clean water, food security, sanitation, and health education and preventative campaigns. "After reviewing the Red Cross' material on mobile health units, it became

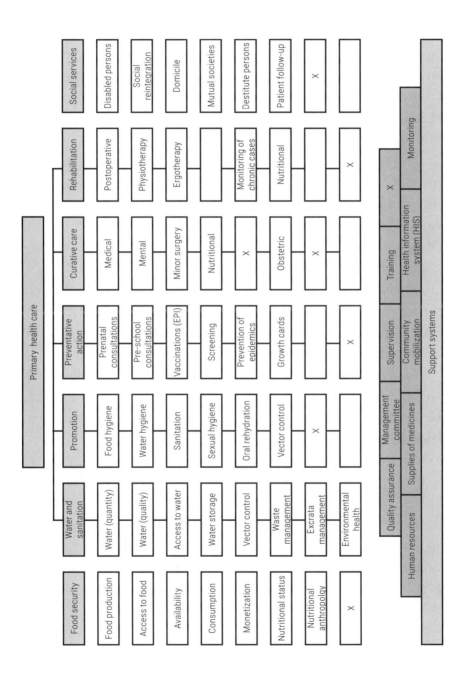

clear that partnering with the government might look different than just delivering direct care. It could encompass promotional and preventative issues, new to Oda but essential to delivering comprehensive health solutions," John says.

Until finding this article and map, John had compartmentalized curative versus preventative care, but this made him recognize that it is a continuum and they are more interrelated.

He also read academic papers about the challenges and promise of remote health clinics. He found a Mobile Outreach Handbook for program planners produced by USAID that outlined a series of successful programs used in mobile clinics. The papers described the challenges the organizations faced and what made their efforts successful, offering a template that Oda could follow.

Moreover, John searched for what kinds of organizations were funding basic healthcare in emerging nations, looked at requirements for applying for donations, and also researched donors to understand their work.

John also identified a group that was doing some work directly with the government, so in his AREA Exploration phase of research, he would reach out to them, ask them about some of their issues, and learn about their experience.

For the drone option, John did a field survey for whether drones were being used for medical kit delivery and the costs involved. John learned that drone operators needed reliable Internet access to pilot their craft. This simply wasn't consistently available in Nepal.

By the end of his AREA "R" research, John had learned a great deal, and his options had shifted. He crafted new theses for his three growth options that were significantly different from his Absolute theses.

1. **Open a second clinic.** Expanding Oda's primary care capacity to a roadside facility would complement our core competencies and serve as a significant lever while we explore

potential growth; however, questions surrounding our ability to recruit and retain competent clinicians remain, as well as the size of the population that would use the facility. Relative data does not conflict with any previous financial assumptions, however, given the continued lack of data and potential downside financial risk, greater clarity is needed on both staffing availability and patient numbers, as well as understanding whether the government will honor its promise to give Oda a building and what kind of capital improvements it might need.

2. Partner with the government in its mobile health units. The Relative research phase uncovered that the government's network is not reliable and that Oda might incur reputational harm by being too closely associated. To work with the government, we would need to have a more distinct and separate role. The research also revealed that education campaigns can be successful for basic health improvements. Perhaps this would enable Oda to work within the system while remaining independent. Oda could consider moving toward prevention rather than treatment, building upon Oda's successful prior campaign to keep girls in school during their period. Yet, the variety of clinics means that we need to explore whether one education campaign might be feasible, or whether Oda would be required to develop multiple campaigns, which might not be feasible given our resources.

3. Use drones to deliver medical kits. By engaging our existing facility, government relationships, and outside partners, we believe drones can effectively supply medicines, diagnostics, specimens, and vaccines to rural Nepal. We believe this concept has long term potential, however, a rapidly changing environment in the drone industry along with the unknowns associated with new technology, reaffirm the importance of finding a partner to offset financial and operational risks. Despite the long-term potential, the lack of reliable Internet in Nepal makes this option currently untenable. Additionally, drone technology has yet to be proven effective in addressing our primary mission, saving lives.

John had a clear path ahead. He made lists of questions that each thesis raised and a detailed list of sources he found from his literature review. What was the real picture according to people he could contact? And how might he best frame his questions to elicit the answers that would be most useful to making a good decision?

Claudia's next steps included talking to students at nursing and coding schools as well as graduates out in the field. She also wanted to talk to employers and understand where the specific opportunities were and what their employees' work days were like. She wanted to confirm that an RN degree would be enough. For coding, she needed a better sense of which schools were good quality and which might be fly-by-night operations. She also wanted to get a sense of how quickly coding language preferences changed and better understand the job and salary outlook. She didn't want to go back to school only to find out that she was learning a language that was on its way out.

Micah wanted to talk to students both currently enrolled at and recently graduated from Pitt and Hopkins. He wanted to find out about how the schools guided students through the pre-med classes, their impression of the professors, and opportunities for undergraduate research. He also wanted to find out whether there was priority acceptance at each university's medical school for its undergraduates. For Pitt, he also needed general medical school acceptance rates.

By completing "R," you've now completed the next concentric circle of information-gathering and are getting a sense of the tension in your target's story. Your Relative research should raise questions that you will want answered in Exploration and your Relative work may help you refine your CCs. Now it's time to road-test your research. Educated and armed with the data you've collected, you're ready to talk to other experts and sources.

4

AREA = E: Exploration

Judge a man by his question rather than his answers.
—Voltaire

There are actually two Es that make up the "E" in AREA: Exploration and Exploitation. They are the twin engines of creativity, one being about breadth of information and the other focusing on depth. One looks for new questions, answers, and understanding, while the other challenges old or accepted certainties.

Each "E" deals with creative ways to upgrade your research beyond the researcher's traditional material by mining the perspective of real people in addition to published sources of material. Exploration and Exploitation are critical components of a quality research process because they direct you to broaden your collection of information and then carefully deepen your ability to distill what you've collected.

This chapter covers Exploration and the following chapter covers Exploitation. In Exploration, I lay out a strategy and method for acquiring new knowledge through developing sources and interviewing. The Exploitation chapter gives you creative tools for some of your own natural mental biases and shortcuts so that you can understand all of the information you've gathered.

Why do you need *more* information? You've gathered data from your target and from the world around your target (your target's landscape/industry, competitors, and the press). You need more information because the real, live people who work for, with, and/or against your target, or write about it, have an important perspective that you can't get on websites or in documents.

This Exploration chapter focuses primarily on investigative journalism techniques that I've honed throughout the years and that will help you get the right information from the right people by asking the right questions. This chapter will teach you:

- How to identify Good Prospects (the right people) to develop sources that many researchers don't or can't find.
- How to get valuable information from your sources by preparing Great Questions.
- How to develop a call/email pitch.
- How to develop an Interview Guide.
- How to conduct targeted interviews so that you feel comfortable interacting with sources, listening and appraising their answers, and taking notes.
- How to evaluate the quality of the information you've collected about your decision so that you can evaluate and flesh out your Critical Concepts.

As Voltaire observed 250 years ago, knowledge is born from great questions. Isaac Newton did not discover gravity because he had the right answers; it's because he asked the right questions.

The goal of this chapter is to give you skills to craft (and an appreciation for) the *right* question for the *right* person so that you may elicit clear, concise, and cogent answers about your Critical Concepts.

Anyone can ask a question, but thoughtful and strategic questions take planning. In this chapter, you'll find the plan to get information that is not available on your research target's website and that hasn't been written about in the *New York Times*. It's the kind of information you can only collect from making a positive connection with another person. It's hard to turn a stranger into a friend via an email or phone conversation, but it's a great way to gain an edge.

Developing Sources and Interviewing

Before getting to the "how" of interviewing, I want to share a story that I think both perfectly illustrates the Exploration process *and* illustrates why this step is key to a thorough research process.

Recently I wrote an investigative news story, published in *Foreign Policy Magazine* and on ProPublica's website, entitled "Can You Fight Poverty With a Five-Star Hotel?" The article reported on the private investing arm of the World Bank, called the International Finance Corporation. The IFC, like the Bank itself, is tasked with fighting poverty in part by spurring economic development. As part of my research, I investigated how the IFC constructed its system for measuring the efficacy of its investments.

I followed my own AREA Research Method and first read Absolute source material documents from the IFC that explained its own system in its own words so that I would not bias myself with outside information. I crafted a thesis statement from the IFC's vantage point, allowing it to speak in its own words.

As part of the process, I read the footnotes of the IFC's Annual Portfolio Review and found that the IFC's measurement system, known as the Development Outcome Tracking System, or DOTS, did not measure the performance of the IFC's actual investments. Instead, it tracked and measured the performance of the *whole company* that received the money, such as The Coca-Cola Company or Newmont Mining.

This illuminating piece of evidence suggested that the IFC might be potentially misleading itself and the public about its investment performance by reporting whole company data. I began the Relative phase of my AREA Method knowing that in both my industry map and in my literature review, I'd look for sources whom I could interview to confirm whether I correctly understood the footnote, whether this was in fact the IFC's current practice, and why the IFC would measure its results this way.

Through my Relative research phase, I put together a list of potential sources (people benefiting from IFC investments, employees at companies that received funds from the IFC, and IFC personnel involved in the DOTS department, for example). I thought about my call pitch, where I outline what I want to say to introduce myself and my topic of conversation, as well as my list of questions and the order of the questions—my Interview Guide—so that I was respectful of my interviewees' time.

I began calling low-level sources who were not critical to my story's success but who fleshed out the IFC's investment measurement system, coached me in how to listen to the answers about the IFC method of evaluation, and better understand how to converse in the IFC's language of operation. Finally, when I was ready to interview my most high-level source for this particular part of my investigation, I reached out to the Chief Results Measurement Specialist and Manager of the IFC's Development Impact Department. During our interview, he explained that once a project is complete, companies generally only track company performance, not project performance, because the latter is difficult to track. Moreover, he acknowledged that some performance indicators only exist at company levels. He described a situation in which a company adds a fifth production line but the company doesn't care about the production of that line. Instead the company cares about the production of all of the lines together.

My interviewee thought he was explaining the IFC's rationale for evaluating its investments as it did, but actually he was telling me that the IFC didn't really know whether its investments were successful because it didn't track the results.

This answer (and others) confirmed two critical things: First, the IFC did not know how successful its investments were because it reported the success of the *entire company* in which the IFC might only have a tiny investment. Second, and equally problematic, was that my interviewee confirmed that the IFC relied on companies' self-reporting and did not do its own due diligence.

In other words, companies the IFC invested in essentially set their own metrics for what would be measured, paid for their own reports, and told the IFC what the results were. Then the IFC used the whole companies' returns on its investments in its tracking system.

Without knowing how its investments fared, how could the World Bank, and countries that support it, know that the Bank was spending its money well and fulfilling its mission of fighting poverty? This question became even more important when further research uncovered that the IFC was increasingly funding investments that did not seem directly tied to its mission of fighting poverty, such as high-end shopping malls, fast food restaurants and, as the title of my story suggests, five-star hotels.

By following the AREA Method, particularly Exploration, I uncovered a financial story that hadn't been told.

But you don't have to uncover a story of financial misrepresentation to benefit from the Exploration stage of AREA. Micah, for example, began his AREA research process with a strong bias in favor of Hopkins based on its reputation and accomplishments. But the Absolute and Relative phases raised serious questions about whether Hopkins was a good fit for him, and uncovered that Pitt had a lot to offer. Micah used his Exploration research to speak to real people and learn about Pitt's pre-med program, professors, and undergraduate research opportunities, while exploring the implications of what he'd learned about Hopkins. Through his Exploration research, Micah uncovered a perspective he hadn't seen previously.

Now it's time to for you to start your Exploration. The first step is to nail the formula.

The Interview Formula: GP + GQ = IQ

The most effective interview is a simple formula: **G**ood **P**rospects plus **G**reat **Q**uestions equals **I**nterview **Q**uality. You identify relevant and interested sources who are qualified to answer your targeted questions, and you ask them the best questions you can formulate to arrive at a quality interview.

Good prospects

How do you find the right people to talk to? That depends on your target's ecosystem and your Critical Concepts. What do you need to know and who out there might know it already? Who knows you, your intentions, and your blind spots? Who might be an expert on you as an interpreter of information and as a decision-maker?

John began his Exploration research with a list of names he culled from his Absolute and Relative research. These Good Prospects were the reporters who wrote articles about the issues he was exploring, as well as the people who had been quoted in those articles. He identified both non-profit experts and health experts in Nepal and other countries. He identified top executives at charities doing similar work around the world, as well as the donors to those causes; he also paid attention to authors of academic papers and speakers at major global healthcare conferences. Finally, he researched the lay leaders in the area of Nepal where his second health clinic might be located, as well as local government officials in the areas that have government clinics.

John searched for the sources' contact information, including LinkedIn, for how he might know or be connected to them. Then he ranked his sources in the order of how useful their information or perspective might be and thought about what kind of information he might glean from them.

John was able to make great contacts through his existing relationships and his Absolute and Relative research, and you will want to start there as well. What are the names that have already popped up in your research?

Cheetah Sheet 11: Finding Good Prospects

1. Industry journals, trade associations, and conferences. Even if you don't attend, some conferences will list speakers and attendees on their web page.

2. Universities and colleges. In addition to professors, PhD students are often easier to reach, and are well versed in critical issues, research, and contacts.

3. LinkedIn. You can search by company/entity to find potential contacts.

4. Industry reporters. Contact them and ask who likes to talk about the industry.

5. Employee unions.

6. Twitter. Search @[company] or @[industry] and see who is talking about the industry.

7. Hoover's and Dun & Bradstreet provide company capsules listing officers and directors of the company and competitors.

8. Lawsuits and the entities named in them, which you can find through court filings.

Who are the people you're looking for as you conduct your search? Insiders who can tell you what the folks who are trying to sell you -on their university or continuing care facility- won't. Claudia found nursing and programming conferences to be great places to get an overview of what was going on in both industries. She didn't even have to pay to be a conference attendee to enter the conferences' exhibition halls, and you might not either since many conferences don't charge anything for people to enter these more public conference spaces. She immediately noticed one thing: At the nursing conference, she saw attendees of all ages and backgrounds. At the computer programming conference, the attendees skewed younger and were heavily male.

As mentioned previously, John talked to employees at charities similar to his own, reached out to academics and experts in basic healthcare delivery systems, and contacted government healthcare employees in Nepal. He also reached out to local community lay leaders and drone technology experts. Sometimes interesting information turns up in unexpected places, including sources that might seem dry at first glance. For example:

1. Experts from other fields.

2. Customers.

3. Alumni of your alma mater who are in the industry.

4. Government and regulatory agencies.

5. Headhunters who cover the industry (their job is networking).

6. Lawyers who have worked for the company or industry.

7. Accountants who specialize in the industry.

8. Strategy consultants.

9. Employees in office departments such as payroll, processing, and IT.

There are three other resources to keep in mind when you need someone to help with a foreign language or when you'd like someone else to help out with your research:

1. Phone companies. Many have translation calling services, which are very helpful if your target speaks a foreign
   language, as many of John's did.

2. Freelance reporters. They can help with finding sources
   and/or conducting interviews. Look on websites such as
   Journalismjobs.com or MediaBistro.com.

3. Librarians.

Also, it is worth identifying interview prospects who are not
necessarily experts on the target or the issue but who are experts on
you, that is, people who deeply understand your interests and values,
default biases, and blind spots. Try to identify one or two people who
know you well and who you'd want to consult as you absorb and
make sense of all the information you gather from other sources.
John, for example, bounced ideas off of the chairman of his board
and one of his key lieutenants.

Valuing your sources

Once you've identified a list of potential sources to contact, write
them down in your AREA journal and rank them in order of the
likelihood that they may provide important information about your
Critical Concepts. Consider what the sources might help you to better understand and then put the sources and put them in order from
least important, or lowest level, to most important.

The lower-level sources can provide you with background and
help you flesh out your understanding of the target, then work your
way up to the sources who you think may provide the most critical
information.

By contacting lower-level sources first, you have a chance to
practice your call pitch, a loose script of what you plan to say to introduce yourself and your task, and to perfect your questions. As
you progress up the interview chain, you will be more polished and
more knowledgeable. Moreover, by the time you've reached your

high-level sources you will not only have a good sense of context, but you will also have a "truth-meter" running that can help guide the way you listen to the answers provided and ferret out incomplete or potentially misleading information.

For example, as you read previously, I thought I knew the answer to the question of how the IFC reported its data before I interviewed my sources. But I didn't want to assume. Having the data enabled me to nicely push back when I received information that I thought might be incomplete. However, it's not time to make these calls yet. First, you need to develop your Great Questions.

Great questions

Before crafting any questions for interviewees, *pause.*

Cheetah Sheet 12: Great Questions Roadmap

1.   What kind of *answers* do I need? These should be targeted on your Critical Concepts.
     a. What do I want to find out and why?
     b. What difference would that information make?

2.   How do I expect to use the information I gather? What would I do if I had an answer to those questions?

If you can't specify how you will use the information before you have it, then there is little reason to expect that you'll figure out how to use it after the findings are in. The goal is to use your time wisely and the time of the people who you reach out to interview.

Next, once you've settled on what you want to know to address your CCs, think about what kind of a response you want to elicit. There are four major kinds of questions that are commonly asked:

1. **Behavior Questions.** What someone does or has done. These kinds of questions will yield descriptions of actual experiences, activities, and actions.

2. **Opinion Questions.** What someone thinks about a topic, action, or event. These questions tell us about people's goals, intentions, desires, and values.

3. **Feeling Questions.** How someone responds emotionally to a topic. These questions elicit information about the emotional responses of people to their experiences and thoughts.

4. **Knowledge Questions.** To find out what factual information the respondent has. These are things that one knows about the research target and your Critical Concepts. You might argue that all knowledge is a set of beliefs rather than facts, but the issue here is to find out what the person being questioned considers to be factual.

In designing your questions, you want to determine precisely what information you need from your interviewee. Do you want to know about their behavior, opinions, feelings, or knowledge? By deciding what is important, you will write questions that clearly communicate to the interviewee what kind of answer you're looking for and avoid confusion.

As with all parts of the AREA Method, think about where and how you might be making assumptions as you write your questions. Often the best questions are the most basic and elemental. Basic does not mean obvious; it means central. It means focused on the Critical Concepts that need to be answered to make your decision.

The following is a classic example of a basic question that made a difference in one money manager's research into an investment opportunity. The manager, a guest speaker in my Advanced Investment Research class, recounted how he was researching a pharmaceutical company whose stock price had soared based on the prospects for an erectile dysfunction gel they were developing. The company had run clinical trials showing that their gel was more effective than a placebo gel applied to a control group. Our guest speaker interviewed people who had seen the research conducted and asked a vital question, one that at first might not be so obvious, and yet turned out to be basic and essential to understanding the study's results: "Who applied the gel to the people in the study?" He learned that while a female applied the company's gel, the placebo gel was applied by a male. The results of the study were indeed statistically significant, but they had nothing to do with the gel.

In terms of what to ask interviewees, many of your questions will come out of the work you've done in the Absolute and Relative phases, and will be specific to your target and decision. However, to help you think about the kinds of questions to ask, I've created a list of good questions that I've learned through the years. These general questions focus on getting interviewees to talk about basic, important qualities regarding an organization.

Cheetah Sheet 13: Great Questions:
Direct, Broad, and Theoretical

Direct questions:

1. How does the entity achieve its goals?

2. What do you think is the most important part of your entity's story?

3. Can you describe an average day? This might include the role he/she plays inside the organization. It reveals the interviewee's priorities. At times, what someone does means more than what the person says.

4. Do you have any concerns about the entity?

Broad questions:

1. What should I know about the industry or sector?

2. Is there a way to bring data to bear on this topic?

Theoretical questions:

1. If you had to do it over again, would you do it differently and how so? Why?

2. If you took money out of the equation, would you still make the same decision, or take the same action? (This question gets beyond the economics of the issue.)

3. Is there more than one possible answer to the previous question?

Claudia interviewed a human resources associate at Montefiore Medical Center. She asked:

1. What positions are open to RNs?

2. What responsibilities do RNs have?

3. Have these responsibilities shifted recently?

4. Do you anticipate another shift coming in the near future?

5. What advice would you give to someone like me, who is considering the field of nursing?

Micah interviewed a student at Pitt and one at Hopkins who were both doing undergraduate medical research. He asked:

1. What requirements did you have to meet to get the research position? How competitive was it to get the position?

2. Who offered support in finding the position and navigating the process? What kinds of support did they provide?

3. How much time does the job require and how much responsibility and supervision do you receive?

4. Would you recommend undergraduate research to someone else?

Once you've written your questions, *pause* and look carefully at the way that you've worded them. The way a question is worded is one of the most important elements in regards to how an interview subject will respond. Are you asking leading questions? Are you providing context for your questions, or simply firing them off one after another? An interviewee will be affected by different question formats.

Micah, for example, really wanted to know whether the undergraduate students he contacted liked the research work they were doing. However, when he reviewed his question list, he felt that asking directly "Do you like the research work you're doing?" was both too pointed and leading, and possibly too personal. He didn't want to put his interviewees on the spot, and the question made it clear that he wanted them to respond with a yes. Would they say yes even if they didn't like their job? Possibly. So he rewrote the question: "Would you recommend undergraduate research to someone else?" This version is softened and has more of an objective tone. Despite the fact that the answer will get the same information—whether the researcher likes her job enough to recommend it to someone else—the question's format has the psychological effect of distance and of allowing the interviewee to be removed from the question. This format might help Micah get more objective and useful information.

Simulation questions provide context in another way: they ask the person to imagine that he or she is in a situation about which the interviewer is interested. Simulation questions you can ask to learn more about an entity's service, product, or process might be:

1. Suppose I was working with you in the clinic/warehouse. What would I see?

2. Describe to me what a typical day is like. What would I see going on?

When Bill and his parents visited The Osborne, Bill's primary concern was getting the pricing information that he'd been unable to find in either in his Absolute or Relative research, but his parents were much more interested in getting a feel for the place. They wanted to speak to residents directly, so they prepared direct, broad, and simulation questions to ask.

Bill and his parents met with a sales manager who gave them a tour. They got some pricing data, but it was a bit overwhelming. After being financially vetted and fulfilling the facility's medical approval, his parents would have to put down a deposit that would start at $800,000—a much higher entry point than the deposit information Bill found from his Absolute numbers research. Each month, residents pay about $5,000, but up to $11,000 for a two-bedroom apartment, with housekeeping and utilities as well as one meal a day. Even if Bill's parents started out paying the low end of the monthly amount, their costs could go up quickly as their needs changed.

There was also a waiting list. Depending on what kind of unit Suzanne and Lester wanted, the wait varied from six month to *10 years*. Even if Bill's parents wanted to live there immediately, they couldn't.

Although the tour gave them pause, they still followed through with their Exploration plan to speak to residents. They asked about a typical day. It gave Bill and his folks a chance to hear about both opportunities and problems that might occur and to understand how a typical day at The Osborne was different than Suzanne and Lester's current daily rhythm. What services were the resident receiving and were they satisfied? Were current residents raising minor or major issues? These questions allowed them to become observers. Bill was taking notes to make a master list of issues that would help him better understand what a routine day might involve. This was valuable in thinking ahead to Analysis, his next step of research in which he'd think about whether the problems raised were solvable.

Make sure to be open and honest when you need clarification. Convey the notion that the need for better understanding is yours, and not a failure of the person being interviewed. You don't want the interviewee to feel inadequate.

It's also important to give the interviewee reinforcement or feedback during the interview. Words of support, thanks, and praise make the person feel appreciated and encouraged. Consider the following clarifying statements or questions to solicit feedback:

1. I'm not sure I follow what you just said. Would you please explain it again?

2. Could you give me an example or anecdote so that I may better understand (or visualize) the concept that you are explaining?

3. It's really useful to have such a clear statement about....

4. I think you are bringing up a lot of important points.

5. I really appreciate your willingness to express your feelings about that. That's really helpful.

The point is to make the interview an interaction, providing stimuli and generating a reaction. To do this, you must be in tune with how the interview is flowing and how the person is reacting to questions.

It's important to maintain control of the interview. Time is precious and sometimes answers may be long-winded, irrelevant, or non-responsive. In order to maintain control, you need to have a sense of what you want to find out and recognize when responses don't provide the right data, so that you get the interviewee back on track. This may take direct feedback. For example, if you ask your interviewee, "What happens when you meet with the sales team?" and she responds, "I try to motivate the team to..." you're getting what she hopes to do or thinks ought to happen. It doesn't describe what actually happens or the techniques she's using in the meeting.

Try reframing the question to get her back on point: "Okay, so you're motivating the team. Take me into the sales meeting. What does the room look like? What would I see and hear? What are you saying?"

Or you might say, "You've explained what you hope to accomplish. Can you describe what you typically do, and what I would see happening if I were there?"

It's hard to interrupt an interviewee. We've all been taught to be polite and not speak when someone else is speaking. However, it's respectful to make good use of the short time available. If the person is long-winded or you are running out of time, you might try reiterating the purpose of your conversation. If you know how much time is allotted at the outset, you can tell the interviewee that time is short, so you might need to interrupt a response to keep the interview moving. For example:

1. "Let me stop you here for a moment. I want to make sure that I fully understand something you touched upon earlier." Then ask a new/more targeted question.

2. "Let me ask you to pause for a moment. I want to come back to what you are saying right now later on in the interview. First I'd like to find out...."

As you ask the questions, write down the number of the question being answered next to the answer so that you know what you've asked without having to note the specific question.

At the end of the interview, ask the interviewee the following questions.

Cheetah Sheet 14: Great Closing Questions

1. What else should I be asking?

2. Who else should I speak to as I continue my research?

3. What organizations do you belong to that might be useful sources of information?

4. What is the best way to follow up with you in the future?

The underlying point of these ideas is that you don't want your wording to limit your responses. You simply want to provide a framework that allows your interviewee to best express his own understanding, in his own terms, so he can select from his full repertoire of responses without bias. The previous discussion provides examples of open-ended (not closed) questions. Refrain from "leading the witness." If you direct the witness, you won't know what he or she might have said.

One way to write a neutral question is to use an illustrative example format, letting the interviewee know that you have pretty much heard it all—the good, the bad, and the ugly—so you're not particularly interested in something sensational; you're really interested in what that person's experience has been like. Bill's questions to residents regarding the food sounded like this: "How do you find the meals? Do you like the variety? When you think about the meals, what comes to mind and how does it impact your happiness here?"

With this format, Bill's series of questions invites a full spectrum of responses. It avoids asking a leading question and gives interviewees permission to elicit a response anywhere on the spectrum.

Ideally you want to ask focused questions that move the interview forward. But this will not be prudent at times, especially once you have hit upon an "aha moment" where you've just received critical information. When that happens, I recommend repeating the question using slightly different words, and/or circling back later in the interview to make sure you understood the answer correctly and there is no ambiguity.

So although every interview should build upon the previous one, expanding on information picked up earlier, moving in a new direction, seeking clarity and elaboration, that doesn't mean always asking different questions to different people. Instead, you may want to have standardized questions so that you ask your interviewees the same questions in the same order.

By following a script that's exactly the same for all interviewees, you can avoid extrapolating from a single anecdote or having a fragmented set of insights. You won't have points all over the place, and you won't falsely derive meaning from a sample of people that is incomplete.

During his Relative research, Micah uncovered negative posts about Hopkins' professors on RateMyProfessor.com. In his Exploration research, he asked every student he spoke to the same questions in the same order so he could see patterns, better appreciate nuance, and spot variation in their answers.

John also used a standard list of questions because he wanted a survey of sorts. In speaking to people who live near government clinics, he wanted to develop a list of questions in which the answers would become a data set.

That said, interview questions will likely need to vary for some individuals based on their vantage points and roles. It may be necessary to alter the questions or wording slightly in order to increase the number of perspectives available.

In addition to considering your questions, I also recommend that you consider the framework for your interviews. There are several kinds of successful interview approaches, but each person ultimately must find a style that feels comfortable to him or her. I outlined a few different interview approaches that are useful at different times:

- **The Scientist.** Here you are value-free, focused single-mindedly on collecting technically sound data. You are an objective scientist on a truth-seeking mission. I usually use this approach with early-stage low-level interviews in which I ask the interviewees to explain how and/or why something is done.
- **The Consultant.** Here you are consensus-building and openly clarifying information. In this approach, you have already collected a lot of data and are partnering with the

interviewee in the search for useful information. I've used this approach with mid-level interviews as a way to share and to check the quality of the information amassed.

- **The Interrogator.** This is a probing, and at times aggressive, style. While thankfully many high-stakes decisions are not adversarial ones, there are times when you are trying to ferret out information by asking some tough questions. If you are the principal at a middle school and there's been a food fight in the cafeteria, this may be the style you need. But for most of the interviews that Bill, Claudia, Micah, and John conducted, an interrogation wasn't necessary.

For Micah, it was jarring to hear that Johns Hopkins had a reputation for weeding out pre-med students. Micah wanted to find out the backstory behind that rumor, and he knew that the admissions people at Hopkins might be defensive or deliberately opaque.

Bill needed to get past the marketing department at the continuing care facilities to learn what the environment was really like. He thought he might need to ask staff members hard and uncomfortable questions based upon the concerns he'd heard from residents.

All three approaches are attractive in their own way and each necessitates a different tone, different word choices, and thoughtful sentence structure. For example, the Scientist style emphasizes truth, so questions should be framed objectively, while the Consultant style emphasizes utility, so questions should be framed analytically. The Interrogator style emphasizes justice and perseverance. Questions are often framed as probing and may include questions that express both fact and opinion. The Interrogator approach should be used sparingly, only after careful consideration and always with sensitivity to the interviewee.

There are two primary ways that I've found the Interrogator style useful and effective. The first is to "back into" the real question that you want to ask. Small revelations make big ones easier, so begin by asking a series of questions that get the interviewee to discuss and confirm small facts that don't seem very controversial. By the time you're ready to ask your main question, the interviewee is, as one might say in a poker game, "pot committed": they've already discussed and divulged information around the main topic, so it's not a leap to move into the real issue that you'd like addressed.

The second way to effectively use the Interrogator style is to simply start in the middle of a conversation. In this style of questioning, you insert facts into your questions, which show you have enough of the material confirmed, so it makes sense for the interviewee to continue the thread of the conversation. For example, in a story I wrote for the Council on Foreign Relations about the U.S. counter-terrorism policies in Africa, I had a government document that criticized parts of the U.S. approach. I knew the subject would be touchy, but I wanted a defense official to address the issues. I used the Interrogator style to present him with my evidence, and it enabled us to have a frank conversation about some of the drawbacks related to our country's counter-terrorism approach.

The idea of figuring out your interview approach and choosing between the Scientist, Consultant, and Interrogator is to determine what kind of information you need. This is similar to the research frames described earlier that allow you to think about your research edges and pitfalls. By assessing what kind of interview approach will work best, you can better build trust, cooperation, goodwill, and interest from the variety of people you need to interview. As you do so, consider that these different styles are mutually beneficial and are not mutually exclusive. By that I mean one or two of these approaches together may better enable you to use the third approach.

For example, although it is logical to follow them in order so that using the Scientist (where you're a straightforward information collector), and then Consultant (where you're seeking consensus), may better enable you to probe as the Interrogator, it also works to use the Scientist and then the Interrogator to make it easier to be the Consultant, which necessitates collaboration and a true sharing of information with your interviewee.

The approach that feels right will be the one that elicits information that is relevant, appropriate, and useful, and that you can't get simply by reading Absolute documents or Relative source material. It's the approach that will yield information about the broader context, the research target, and a specific set of issues and questions vital to your Critical Concepts.

Claudia realized through her Relative research that she might need more than an initial round of retraining; she might need ongoing education and training in either of the fields she was contemplating. She realized that both fields were more in flux than she expected. So she developed an interview script and list of questions to investigate this particular issue. She reached out to human resource departments at the hospitals in her area as well as companies advertising for software and data scientists, industry experts, and current and former employees of the hospitals and companies in her search. One interviewee told her, "I'm constantly reading industry journals to keep up on the latest changes, and I realize that I need to find time to go to industry conferences and training seminars every year so that [my employer] knows I'm up to date. They expect me to keep up."

This insight confirmed what she suspected based on her Relative research: although both computer programming and nursing were growing fields, they were constantly experiencing change. She learned she had too rosy a picture of the fields at the outset. She needed to evaluate how she felt about her decision with this new understanding that both options offered more volatility than she'd thought.

Micah, unable to find any statistical information about Pitt's pre-med program in Absolute and Relative, finally got this information in the Exploration research phase when he spoke with a dean in the Honors College. She told him that about 25 percent of Pitt students who attend the mandatory freshman year pre-med information session completed the medical school requirements, a slightly higher finish rate than at Hopkins. She also told him that many of the students who came to the information session were not strongly committed to pre-med; Pitt has programs in many other health care areas, including nursing, dentistry, EMT training, and medical research, and many freshmen switched to one of these other fields early on. However, of the Pitt students applying to medical school, only 59 percent were accepted, a significantly lower number than Hopkins. The dean emphasized that students who worked with the pre-med advising office had an acceptance rate of 79 percent, almost identical to Hopkins.

This last data point made Micah reassess his Critical Concepts because he understood that Pitt's pre-med advising office was a critical gateway to improving students' medical school acceptance rates. He'd assumed all along that he would have an advisor at any school he attended. But he spoke with a few students at Hopkins about the advisory system and found consistently disappointing news: the staff was overwhelmed with all the premed students and not available to provide one-on-one help with course planning or with developing a list of medical schools. Hopkins also strongly encouraged students to apply to medical school during their senior year, rather than in their junior year. This meant Micah would need to use his senior year to do all the steps required to apply and then take a gap year between college and medical school. He also learned that there was less preparation offered by Hopkins advisory staff when it came to mock interviews. In contrast, the guidance at Pitt seemed much more available, helpful, and effective.

Finally, to follow up on the RateMyProfessor.com information, Micah asked Hopkins students about the comments he'd read on the site. The students mostly didn't use that website; instead, they asked around about a professor's reputation (possibly something that was harder to do at a large school like Pitt). However, their assessments of the professors weren't reassuring. One student said, "I don't think they were great professors. They're leading researchers in the field, so a standard chemistry equation for them is like tying their shoes. They don't wrap their head around that we're freshmen and we don't understand the material. At Hopkins, you learn how to learn on your own."

Micah believed he was a good student, and he knew how to study. But he wasn't sure he wanted to go to college to learn on his own.

Timing Your Interviews

It seems that we're all overbooked these days. Be mindful of that as you reach out to interrupt someone else's day to benefit your own. In other words, a critical factor in making a good question list is a consideration for how much time you think you may actually get with a person. If you think you may only have 15 minutes, make a comprehensive list of questions and then whittle it down to the most essential ones that will collect the information that you require to better examine your target's Critical Concepts. Make each question necessary, clear, and concise, and move the interview forward from the prior one.

Cheetah Sheet 15: Vetting Your Great Questions

1. Are you writing the same question in multiple forms and being repetitive?

2. Are there extraneous questions that you may delete?

3. How can you improve the clarity of your questions?

Assess what you really need to have answered in the time allotted and prioritize your questions so that you cover the most important elements.

The Interview Guide

Once you've developed a list of Great Questions, it's time to *pause* and create your Interview Guide. How do you want to the interview to proceed? What are the most important questions you need answered? What follow-up questions will be important to ask based on the answers you get?

An Interview Guide is a roadmap that lays out the framework for the interview so that you can control the timing and momentum, and navigate the path to make sure you're able to ask your most critical questions in the time you will have with your interview subjects.

Figure out a good logical progression for your topics and subject areas to extract the right information. A good Interview Guide does not necessarily follow only a straightforward logical progression. It should follow the tributaries of a natural conversation, which is less formal and meant to put less distance between you and your interviewee than a classic interview might.

The guide should house your specific open-ended questions, vetted for tone, bias, and clarity so that the questions are worded closely to the way they will be asked. The Guide serves as a basic checklist during the interview to make sure that all relevant topics are covered in a thoughtful way, and it also ensures that you are able to easily compare information across your interviews covering the same material.

Of course, once you've crafted your Guide, you may adapt both wording and sequencing of questions to specific interviewees in the context of the actual interview. You may also want to build conversation within specific subject areas, develop spontaneous questions, and establish a conversational style with the careful focus on a particular predetermined subject.

To make your Interview Guide compelling and to craft a logical progression for your interview so that it best resembles the normal flow of conversation, it's useful to have your questions follow a storyboard with a beginning, middle, and end.

Cheetah Sheet 16: Storyboarding Your Great Questions

1. Begin with an introduction that explains who you are, what you are researching, and why.

2. Open with some non-confrontational, non-controversial, and easy-to-discuss questions that have concrete answers.

3. Lead into your Critical Concept questions—the meat of your concerns about your decision.

4. Wrap up the conversation with the final questions: "What haven't I asked?" and "What am I missing?" Thank the interviewee, ask how to get back in touch for any follow-up, and ask for recommendations of other people to contact for your research.

Recognize that if you do not build a storyboard for your questions, they may seem abrupt, unnatural, and potentially off-putting. People generally like to talk about their work, but in order for them to truly share their thoughts, feelings, and evidence, they need to get comfortable with you—a stranger—whether the interview is being conducted over the phone, in person, or via email. From a journalist's perspective, it's always better to speak to someone directly, but many people are comfortable with email.

The key thing is to put yourself in the place of the interviewee and consider how you and your questions might come across to a stranger. Before conducting the interview, imagine being on the receiving end of the questions. Thoughtful questions are sensitive to the intrusion being made into your source's life and sensitive to the good will needed to obtain valid and useful responses. Sensitivity and clarity go together.

The underlying theme: Have an idea of what you want to find out and then design questions, and the order that they will be asked, to give you the information you think you need. *You have a better chance of getting good information if you are able to conceptualize and structure your interviews well.*

If you're going to be speaking or meeting with the person, rehearse your interview. How do your questions sound out loud? Put some evidence of your research into your questions so that the interviewee knows you've done some work and that you have some familiarity with the issues. This gives them confidence that you are not wasting their time, and it will better enable you to have a conversation, not just an interview, because you will show that you can share data and insights.

Finally, to help make a connection with your interviewees, conduct background research on each person you intend to contact. Your goal in this research phase isn't to learn *everything* there is to know about your interviewee but to find *something* in common that will help you build rapport and give you better insight into the interview subject. Your research may be a basic Internet, Facebook, and LinkedIn search to see whether your interviewee has written articles, where she may have been quoted, and what personal interests she may have that will allow an easier introduction.

People like to be noticed. If you can notice your interviewee's accomplishments, or show him you've taken the time to learn something about him before calling, he will likely be flattered. For example, when John wanted to speak with Dr. Miriam Cremer, who heads up Basic Health El Salvador, he let her know he was aware of the work she had done and saw parallels to his work in Nepal. He also mentioned that their organizations were both operating in similar environments, in countries with governments facing big challenges, and made sure to say that her organization was several years ahead of his so he felt he could learn from her.

The advantage of the Interview Guide is that you've made sure you have carefully decided how best to use the limited interview time available. It allows you to assume that you may only get this one chance to speak with the person you are reaching out to, even if she says you may call her again.

Moreover, an organized guide makes data analysis much easier because it is possible to locate each respondent's answer. And it allows for replication: If you or someone else wants to check your work, they will know what was previously asked. The goal is to guarantee that the interviews are relevant, appropriate, consistent, and useful.

Interviewing

Congratulations! Now you're ready to start interviewing. Essentially, conducting an interview is about multi-tasking. It is much more than just listening. It requires interacting easily with people, generating rapid insights, taking notes both on the conversation you're having and on your interview guide, and formulating new questions quickly while guarding against asking questions that impose interpretations on the situation, *and* reading clues, such as tone and pauses, to respond to what is not being said.

If you think it's tiring just to read this, know that it is even more tiring to conduct a successful interview. Don't conduct an interview on an empty stomach, and make sure that the time you allot for the interview includes time for your "after-interview" process, which should immediately follow the end of the formal interview.

Once you are ready, the first challenge is to get your interview target on the phone. This is where a considerate call pitch comes in. What is the short "elevator speech" that you plan to use?

Although there is no one right way to conduct an interview, I recommend that in this brief speech, you achieve three things: be educated, be compelling, and be urgent in your cause. You need the person to speak with you now, or soon. Write your intro speech out and rehearse it. Here is one of the call pitches John used:

> Hi, I'm John, the founder of the Oda Foundation, a charity based in a rural region of Nepal that provides basic health-care services. I'm reaching out to you because I noticed that your organization provides a similar service in Sub-Saharan Africa and I'm considering expanding our health services to include a new urban clinic. I'd like to ask you about (your first topic). Have I reached you at a good time?

If the time you called doesn't work, make a date for something that works at the source's convenience, stressing that you are flexible and can work with your source's busy schedule.

In the example, John not only explains who he is but also what his organization does, where, and exactly why this person is relevant to his research. It shows he has done work before picking up the phone, making it more likely that the person will talk with him, feeling that he's not going to waste the interviewee's time. Now that you are ready to make calls, be patient and have confidence in yourself. It may take a while to get someone to speak with you.

In my experience, only about one in four calls will result in an interview (if you're lucky). It's a numbers game. So expect to get rejected. Develop a thick skin and remember: the more calls you make, the more interviews you'll get.

People will take your call if they think there is something in it for them. Many people like to talk about work, so feeling like someone has a genuine interest in what they do can be exciting. Keep in mind, however, that employees at different levels have different experiences. If you're talking to a low-level employee, understand what it feels like to have a boss coming down on you. If you're talking to a mid-level contact, appeal to her desire to help and her desire to feel important. If you're talking to a high-level contact, showing that you're well-versed in your topic may yield deeper conversation.

Once you have someone on the phone, remember the sage advice given by Zeno of Citium in 300 BC: "We have two ears and one mouth so we should listen more than we say." Although this is difficult, it is important to recognize that different people have different styles of speaking, and you will do best if you learn to adjust to each of your interview subject's personal mannerisms. Leading a good interview takes practice. It is not just about data collection, it is also about interaction and relationship-building. The purpose of interviewing is to find out what is on someone else's mind. It is not to put new ideas into someone's mind, but to access the perspectives of the person being interviewed.

Keep in mind that we usually interview to find out things we cannot directly observe, such as feelings, thoughts, and intentions (sometimes interviews may be to confirm or rebut what we have observed, but more on that later). We want to enter into the other person's perspective because it is meaningful, knowable, and accessible.

Interviews provide insights you can't develop on your own, confirmation of data and information you've already gathered, and a deeper understanding of how something works, or why it works the way it does.

It's the interviewer's responsibility to provide a framework within which people may respond comfortably, accurately, and honestly to open-ended questions. The quality of the information obtained is largely dependent upon the interviewer.

Thus, while you want to rapidly get down to business to accomplish the necessary tasks, you really want to be both sufficiently directive to get the job done *and* sufficiently non-directive and open to allow interview subjects to feel that their inputs are meaningful and substantive. You want to unlock and stimulate conversation in the people you are speaking with and then figure out how to be reactive, adapting to the conversation as it progresses.

If you are conducting a face-to-face interview, notice the interviewee's demeanor. Is she friendly and comfortable? Does she seem nervous? If so, perhaps you've stumbled upon a topic that the person is uncomfortable with, or one in which the interviewee wants to say more but is hesitant or still formulating her thoughts.

Whether you are interviewing in person or on the phone, I recommend not interrupting a pause, and allow the silences to hang so that the interviewee can to fill it. Allow the interviewee to decide how to fill her silences.

Taking Notes

If possible, wear a headset when conducting a phone interview. This will prevent your interviewee from hearing you type while he is speaking, which can be uncomfortable. You don't want to put the keyboard between you and your source; it changes the call from a natural conversation to an interview.

If the interviewee is speaking too quickly, slow down the interview. Try either repeating what the person said as you write it down, or asking her to repeat it. You might also consider saying, "May I have a minute? You made an important point there, and I want to make sure that I have it down in my notes."

I also find it valuable to develop shorthand. I often just drop the vowels so that I can type faster. Some important conventions along this line to consider are:

1. Only use quotation marks during note-taking to indicate full and actual quotations.

2. Develop a system to indicate interpretation, thoughts, or ideas that occur. For example, I use brackets to set off my own ideas from the interviewee. I use the margins to record non-verbal notes such as whether the person seems angry about a specific issue, or seems to know more than he or she may be indicating.

3. Keep track of the questions you ask as they are answered by writing down the number of the question as it corresponds to the number on your Interview Guide.

You may be tempted to record some of your interviews. However, be aware that one-way recording is only allowed in some states. Check the rules for yours. And even if you do record, take notes. Note-taking is active listening and a filtering system. Taking notes by hand or typing them makes it easier to locate something someone said in the tape of the interview, and will facilitate future analysis. Another important benefit of taking written notes is that sometimes even the best recording systems fail; it's always good to have a manual backup.

If you are recording and taking notes, write the start time of the interview on the top of your notes, then every 15 minutes or so record the time code in the margin.

When the interview is over, immediately take a few quiet minutes to read through all of your notes. Use this "after-interview" time to make sure that you've recorded the number of the question next to the corresponding answer and to fill in and flesh out answers that you recorded quickly while the interview is still fresh and you can record more comprehensively.

Be careful to note if you change or add things that may not accurately reflect exactly what the interviewee said during the interview, so that you don't confuse what was said in the interview with your notes after it. Record your impressions of how and why the person said what he said in important places. Indicate if you thought someone was not being fully truthful or forthcoming and why you had that impression, or if, through verbal and non-verbal cues, someone seemed worried about sharing certain information with you. By staying with the interview after it's over and reading your notes immediately, you will be surprised at how different the notes may be from what you thought they were.

Always add your interview sources to your list of contacts for future follow-up, along with notations about the content of the call and how useful the interview was. In so doing, you will have a better context for knowing how and when to call upon the person in future Explorations, and you will be able to remind the person when you last spoke and what you discussed. Note any recommendations for future contacts so that you may recall their other connections in the future. And of course send a thank-you note or email. This leaves your interaction in a good place.

Finally, *pause* and develop a thesis statement from your interviews.

Once John had identified his Good Prospects, he crafted a list of questions that would check, verify, and flesh out information he collected in Absolute and Relative as well as collect new information. Then he set about interviewing. He conducted about half a dozen interviews, mostly on the phone, although one was via email and another was in person.

In the following excerpt from John's interview, he spoke with one of Oda's on-the-ground clinicians and the district health officer, Doctor Shankar Lohala. These are John's notes from those conversations, not direct quotes. He underlined the answers that had significance and pointed his way forward in his research.

Q: Is the government building still being offered to Oda (permission given six months ago)?

A: Yes, a letter was signed by the District Government and Pili Government confirming that when/if we decide to work in this facility, we will not have problems.

Q: What is the Condition of the Building? How much time/efforts/funds would be necessary prior to moving basic supplies and material in?

A: Structurally the building is in fine shape; with cosmetic changes, it would be available for basic operations.

Q: Would more people come to the facility from outside of Kalikot?

A: Likely yes, in what amount not sure.

Q: How many people would use the new facility rather than Oda?

A: Not sure, when talking to Oda team, however, they agreed that there would be materially more patient volume.

Q: Are there any major financial differences between Oda Facility and Pili?

A: If we continue to focus on primary health care with no real advanced capabilities, then the only real financial difference would be volume.

Q: Partnering with the government option: would the government still endorse this?

A: Yes, According to the District Health Officer this is the preferred choice for the government as we plan.

Q: Would the community be cooperative if Oda partnered with the government?

A: <u>No way to say with certainty, this is one of the major focuses of the circuit. Who is responsive/engaged, what are needs, etc.</u>

Q: What issues should be addressed in the health education side of things? What should we do and why?

A: Doctor Shankar wants to discuss, agrees that focus on maternal and adolescent issues would be good.

The interview revealed that opening a second clinic and partnering with the government were supported by the government. But in opening a second clinic, patient volume was a big unknown. His interviewee said twice that he didn't know how many patients would visit a roadside clinic, but he knew it would be more than Oda was currently serving. It became clear that patient volume was a significant question mark. With regards to the outreach option, John learned that although the District Health Office would support the initiative, there was no way to be sure of grassroots support at the government clinics.

He came to two important insights from his interviews. The first was informational. His interviews made him much more comfortable that a roadside clinic was viable and that the government's health clinics were both problematic and diverse. By speaking to the District Health Officer and a local medical assistant who had been in a few of the clinics, he learned that the government's clinics were not comparable to one another. Some were better staffed or had problems with medical supplies, some faced one kind of disease outbreak, while others treated a variety of illnesses. The clinic's issues were hyper-local. He realized that partnering with the government and using its health network to conduct an education campaign was much trickier than initially understood. John also confirmed that the drone option was going to be untenable in the short term.

His second insight, no less important, was behavioral, and was something that he could only get from interviewing. He read his interviewees verbal and non-verbal clues. Most of the people he spoke with who worked for the Nepalese government health system were downtrodden in their tone and word choice. He did not get a sense that the head of Nepal's district healthcare system really knew what was happening in each clinic, or what their day-to-day experience was like. He did not have confidence that the individuals making decisions actually knew that their directions were being implemented, or if they were implemented, and if it was in a consistent and high-quality way.

The depth of understanding that John gained through AREA Exploration was a game-changer. He could not have understood this reality either from the Absolute research he did, reading what Nepal's government disclosed about its clinics, or from Relative, which more broadly gave him information about some problems, but hadn't illuminated the specific differences between clinics or how the communities felt about them.

His thesis statement from his Exploration interviews read:

My interviews indicate that a second clinic is viable and realistic and would be welcome in the community, although the building being offered needs much more rehabilitation than previously expected. That would mean needing to raise more money than expected and would delay expanding our services by almost nine months. Exploration interviews also reveal that traffic at a roadside clinic may be much heavier than anticipated and there may be a more diverse and perhaps more serious set of illnesses than we've cared for in the past, raising concern about our ability to be effective both financially and operationally. Moreover, the government has expressed a clear preference that we work with their network of clinics instead of opening our own roadside facility.

Partnering with the government is more problematic than initially understood in three ways: First it might entail Oda developing several different education campaigns instead of a single comprehensive program because the clinics seem to have different needs; second, it revealed that the government official in charge of the healthcare system does not have a clear picture of the day-to-day reality of all of the clinics; and third, it is unclear what expectation the government has for the education campaigns and this needs to be clarified. This again raises the issue of whether Oda might be able to work with the clinics to deliver a preventative care education campaign instead of treatment. If Oda can maintain its independence, this might be a solution.

Exploration research confirmed that drones require an available Internet connection at the base and receiving locations, which is not available in many areas of Nepal and is not currently viable.

John concluded from his thesis statement that his Critical Concepts were evolving. From his five original CCs, he was down to only three as his research sharpened his understanding of what he really needed to know to make his decision about Oda's growth strategy:

1. **Buy-in.** Did Oda have buy-in from both the government and the community for both options? It was not sufficient to only have buy-in from one of his two constituencies. The government wanted him to pursue a partnership, but what was the community's experience with the government's clinics? He needed to move beyond anecdotes to examine the risk of the government's poor reputation.

2. **Ability to execute.** Did Oda have the operational capacity to succeed in both options?

3. **Financial efficacy.** What would be the impact per dollar spent? John could define that in a few different ways. Might it be the number of patients treated, or the number of girls who attended an education seminar about menstrual care? Or might it assess how many girls increased their school attendance after attending the education seminar?

Like John, you should be able to further refine your Critical Concepts from the work you've done in Exploration. The next step is "E" representing Exploitation. The research moves from the outside world to evaluate your own thinking and where your research might have gone amiss.

5

AREA = E: Exploitation

Habit is habit, and not to be flung out of the window,
but coaxed downstairs a step at a time.

—Mark Twain

Read the following paragraph:

Aoccdrnig to rscheearch at Cmabridge Uinvervtisy, it deosn't mttaer in waht oredr the ltteers in a wrod are, the olny iprmoetnt tihng is taht the frist and lsat ltteer be at the rghit pclae. The rset can be a ttoal mses and you can sitll raed it wouthit a porbelm. Tihs is besauae ocne we laren how to raed we bgien to aargnre the lteerts in our mnid to see waht we epxcet to see. The huamn mnid deos not raed ervey lteter by istlef, but preecsievs the wrod as a wlohe. We do tihs ucnsoniuscoly wuithot tuhoght.

You're finding meaning in a mass of jumbled letters. Surprising, isn't it? How is this possible? When information enters the mind, it self-organizes. New information fits itself into existing experiences and familiar patterns. Even if much of the information is new, the mind will default to patterns previously activated and automatically "correct" and "complete" the information received.

In the sample paragraph, your brain takes a bit of information (the first and last letters) and activates the "word" channel, and you see and understand the word. This is why when we try to have new ideas or solutions, we often come up with the same familiar ideas. Information flowing down the same channels, making the same old connections, produces the same old ideas over and over again. Our brains are almost like personal judicial systems, making decisions based upon precedents. We have a (well-meaning) incentive *not* to learn new things.

The AREA Method readily acknowledges our cognitive shortcomings and is crafted to help you identify the source and perspective of your information, so that you can not only develop a healthy skepticism about the information you gather, but also spot new or dis-confirming data. Noting that all information is influenced by its authors, the second section of "E" moves from Exploration, which broadens your research by listening to others, to Exploitation, which evaluates *your* perspective and understanding of your information and ideas.

The exercises in Exploitation are meant to break down your information and your thought processes so that you can study the elements and structure of both. It will help you *evaluate* your work and then ascribe *value* to it, while closely reining in your cognitive short cuts. It may lead you to collect more information and to do more work.

In the next chapter, Analysis, you will process the data you've gathered, interpreting it all and taking a final Cheetah Pause to ask, "What does it all mean?"

Evaluation and interpretation are two discrete ways of thinking that we often combine into one. Evaluation is an assessment of something. Interpretation is your opinion on what it means. By separating them, the AREA Method challenges us to slow down and to think about our thinking. At the end of the Analysis chapter, you will again have to rely upon your own judgment.

To begin the evaluation phase, Exploitation provides you with a set of creative tools and techniques that come from experts in journalism, intelligence-gathering, medicine, and psychology. These tools will help you improve your analytical skills and will protect you from avoidable errors of bias that impede sound decision-making about your data. Our instinct to piece things together from incomplete information can be both good and bad, but in making a high-stakes decision, we want to avoid the bad.

The goal is to gain new insights, original ideas, and solutions. Insight comes when new information enters the brain and connects with information previously stored there to craft a new understanding. It may be achieved by active study or by presence of mind. The exercises in Exploitation will help you to achieve insight by activating these connections. These creative exercises are meant to:

- Identify flaws in the way you're educated to trust your judgment.
- Encourage you to connect dots and derive insights across your research.
- Promote thinking beyond the boundaries of already established fact.

Remember: The truth can rarely be reduced to certainties. The following exercises embrace uncertainty to lead us toward a clear, insightful appraisal of the situation. As Central Intelligence Agency analyst Richards Heuer wrote in his book *Psychology of Intelligence Analysis*, "Major intelligence failures are caused by failures of analysis, not failures in data collection."

The way that Heuer and others teach us to prevent such failures is *not* to simply confirm things that you already believe, but to *disconfirm* them instead.

One prominent method of disconfirmation is something many of us learned in an early science class: the scientific method. Dating back to the 17th century, the scientific method teaches scientists to prove that they can't reject their hypotheses rather than trying to prove that they can confirm them. It has four simple steps:

1. Define a problem.

2. Formulate an educated guess or hypothesis.

3. Design an experiment to test the hypothesis.

4. Analyze the results.

Like the scientific method, the goal of the exercises in this chapter is to provide an objective, standardized approach to testing hypotheses that minimizes the influence of bias. You have already created several hypotheses with your thesis statements from Absolute, Relative, and Exploration. In this chapter, you will develop and test additional hypotheses to move your research story forward by scaffolding onto earlier hypotheses, in the same way a scientist follows the scientific method to refine her hypothesis. By using a standardized approach to investigate your hypotheses, you will have better comfort and confidence that you can stick to the facts and limit the influence of personal, preconceived notions.

Yet even with such a rigorous methodology in place, we still make mistakes from time to time. We might fail to accurately account for errors, such as problems with measurement or data selection, or we may mistake a hypothesis for a factual statement. For example, think of the terrible mistake made in 2003 when the United States invaded Iraq based on the Bush administration's assertion that the country was stockpiling weapons of mass destruction. This was not a statement of fact, but rather a hypothesis.

What's more, a theory may be correct without foolproof evidence. For example, the theory of relativity predicted the existence of black holes long before there was actual evidence of black holes.

However, one of the goals of science—and of this section—is to try and disprove a theory even when you think you are on to something.

The key point is to focus not only on finding information that confirms your hypotheses, but also on demonstrating that you can't disconfirm them. It's a more robust process that will lead to fewer errors. Having 20 reasons to follow a certain path may not matter if there are two insurmountable roadblocks.

Charlie Munger, the vice-chairman of Berkshire Hathaway, is fond of using such techniques and has been known to say "Invert, always invert." By inverting our thinking, we take conscious control of it. This may sound easy, but it's hard to do in practice because we are *wired* to jump to conclusions.

What follows is a discussion of four exercises to help you question your thinking and your data. Although you may want to pick and choose among the exercises and the various ways to view the evidence you've gathered, these exercises are not interchangeable. Rather, they are interrelated. They work to get you out of your own perspective. They are channel blockers that push your thinking and decision-making habits out of their well-worn pathways and into new patterns. Ideally, each exercise allows you to see your decision in a new light, so that you build a layered understanding of your decision. For this reason, this chapter follows John through all of the exercises to see how they work together to bring him to a new understanding of his options.

The Competing Alternative Hypotheses (CAH) Exercise

The Competing Alternative Hypotheses (CAH) exercise was developed by Richards Heuer, a 45-year veteran of the CIA. In the 1970s, Heuer ran the agency's methodology unit in its intelligence operations department. During his tenure, Heuer realized that most CIA errors were not the result of insufficient data, but rather insufficient ability to process data correctly because of human biases. He penned the manual *Psychology of Intelligence Analysis,* which details some of his thinking about problems of human perception and their manifestation in analytical errors.

Heuer believed that we all face inherent difficulties in processing complex information, but analysts could offset these psychological shortcomings by creating a system to manage them. In developing the CAH exercise, Heuer wanted to provide researchers with an unbiased process of analysis to avoid some common analytical pitfalls like ignoring evidence that conflicts with an existing hypothesis or rejecting an alternative hypothesis without thorough evidence. By forcing you to systematically work through evidence and its implications, CAH avoids the errors of oversight that occur in a bias-influenced process. Furthermore, like the Cheetah Pauses where you craft your thesis statements, CAH leaves an audit trail.

Two key elements distinguish CAH from conventional analysis. First, CAH starts with a full set of hypotheses rather than the most likely hypothesis for which you seek confirmation. By laying out all of your hypotheses and data together, CAH systematically evaluates the impact of each data point against each hypothesis. By giving all hypotheses equal time and attention, you keep from succumbing to bias. You won't only match evidence against what you deem to be your most likely hypothesis. This ensures that alternative hypotheses receive equal treatment and a fair shake. For though you may get lucky and have an imprecise analytic approach work out well, using CAH enables you to ferret out key connections between data and hypotheses that are not always obvious or intuitive. You don't want to run roughshod over an unexpected insight.

Second, though conventional analysis generally entails looking for evidence to confirm a favored hypothesis, CAH identifies and zeros in on data points that can support multiple hypotheses, which means that those data points may not be as useful as initially expected. A data point that supports a particular hypothesis might seem compelling, but if it supports every hypothesis, it actually has very little diagnosticity. Something that is true is unlikely to have disconfirming data but something that is untrue might have supporting information. Thus in CAH, it's more important to focus on the negatives than the positives. The result is that the most probable hypothesis is usually the one with the least evidence *against* it, not the one with the most evidence for it.

Initially, John thought having opened one successful clinic was a strong data point for opening a second health clinic. As he went through CAH, he realized that knowing how to successfully provide healthcare supported *both* of his hypotheses; it was a positive indicator that he could have success with a second clinic *and* have success partnering with the government. As a result, the data point about having a successful clinic had little diagnosticity.

Thus the CAH exercise discourages you from what decision scientists call "satisficing," or picking the first solution that seems satisfactory, rather than going through all of the possibilities to identify the best solution. Although it might be of small consequence to "satisfice" when choosing, say, a particular brand of cream cheese at the grocery store, it can be very costly to do so when the decision will affect your earning potential and job satisfaction for years to come.

By going through all possible solutions, you're less likely to be led astray by trying to confirm only one hypothesis that you think is true. You won't run the risk of having just enough evidence to support a favored hypothesis while failing to recognize that most of that evidence is also consistent with other hypotheses. You may also bring to light previously unconsidered ways of interpreting evidence.

In focusing more attention on alternative explanations, CAH brings out the full uncertainty inherent in any situation that is, in Heuer's words, "poor in data but rich in possibilities." Such uncertainty can be frustrating, but is likely a more accurate reflection of the true situation. As Voltaire said, "Doubt is not a pleasant state, but certainty is a ridiculous one."

By focusing attention on the few items of critical evidence that cause the uncertainty (or if they were available, would alleviate it), the CAH exercise can guide future collection, research, and analysis to resolve the uncertainty and produce a more accurate judgment.

The CAH process has eight steps grounded in basic insights from cognitive psychology and decision analysis. Subsequent discussion can then focus productively on the ultimate source of the differences. For a detailed explanation of the following outline, you can go to areamethod.com. For now, the following Cheetah Sheet contains a quick outline to help you get started.

Cheetah Sheet 17: Step-by-Step Outline for CAH Exercise

1. Identify the possible hypotheses that merit detailed examination.

2. Make a list of significant evidence and arguments for and against each hypothesis.

3. Prepare a chart with hypotheses across the top and evidence down the side. Analyze the evidence against each hypothesis. Identify which pieces of evidence confirm each hypothesis, which are disconfirming, and which may need more research to be able to tell whether they confirm or disconfirm the hypotheses.

4. Refine the chart. Reconsider the hypotheses and delete evidence and arguments that have no diagnostic value.

5. Draw tentative conclusions about the relative likelihood of each hypothesis. Proceed by trying to disprove the hypotheses rather than prove them.

6. Analyze how sensitive your conclusion is to a few critical items of evidence. Consider the consequences for your analysis if that evidence were wrong, misleading, or subject to a different interpretation.

7. Report conclusions. Discuss the relative likelihood of all the hypotheses, not just the most likely one.

8. Identify milestones for future observation that may indicate events are taking a different course than expected.

This exercise requires you to clearly delineate your assumptions. Micah had two competing hypotheses:

1. Pitt will enable me to successfully get to medical school.

2. Hopkins will enable me to successfully get to medical school.

He came up with the hypotheses based on having his heart set not on college but on medical school. Initially he had five pieces of evidence that he tested against the two hypotheses:

1. Percentage of students who complete pre-med requirements

2. Percentage of pre-med students accepted to medical school.

3. Selectivity of medical schools.

4. Undergraduate research opportunities.

5. Debt at graduation.

As he began completing the CAH chart, he realized that the selectivity of the medical school didn't really matter if he wasn't going to be able to complete the pre-med requirements. The numbers were stacked against him: nationally, far more students fail to complete the pre-med requirements than complete them. Hopkins's 80 percent wash-out rate was high, but not much higher than Pitt's 75 percent.

How could Micah beat these odds? He started to think about the best way to ensure that he would get through his pre-med courses: He wanted good professors who taught the material, he wanted to feel supported by his advisor, and wanted to feel that the advisor would be available for him. When he thought about the decision in these terms, and added in the costs of his two options, he arrived at an unexpected answer: Micah accepted University of Pittsburgh.

Although the AREA Method has more steps, Micah skipped forward from the CAH to the Analysis part of his process. CAH was such a game-changer for him that he didn't need more Exploitation exercises.

John's CAH pointed back into earlier steps to do more work— work that he diligently completed and that ultimately changed his understanding of Oda's growth options.

Oda Foundation CAH exercise

		Competing Alternative Hypotheses	
		Roadside Clinic expands service with positive health outcomes	Government Health Network and education campaign improves long-term health outcomes and preventative care.
E	Donated Facility	+	NA
C	Grassroots Support for Project	+	+/?
N	Access to Government Network	NA	+/?
E	Condition of Facility	-	NA
D	Medical Staff Available (Jagat)	+	+
—	Previous Successful Education Campaign	+	+
>	Patient Numbers/ Illnesses at Roadside Location	?	NA
E	Previous Successful Clinic	+	+

As you can see, there were many positives for both the roadside clinic and partnering with the government, but by completing CAH, John knew the positives didn't matter: it was the negatives he needed to pay attention to, and he couldn't yet identify what the true negatives were because he was missing some key data.

He identified three factors (those shaded in gray), that were going to be the most critical factors in determining which decision he made. For the government partnership option, he didn't know if the local communities would be receptive to an Oda partnership and he didn't know how much of a negative it was to be associated with the government. For the second clinic option, he didn't have any good data about the patient volume the clinic would be serving.

Each of these issues could make or break Oda's ability to expand successfully. By being diligent and thoughtful and writing out his CAH, he realized that he needed to collect the data that would support or disconfirm the three factors he still had questions about.

For the second clinic, he needed data about patient volume and the common illnesses it would be treating. For the government partnership option, he needed data about community acceptance and whether Oda could maintain independence while working within government clinics. Pinning these factors down would enable John to determine whether either option was viable.

"The exercise really crystallized what to focus on," says John. "It identified what targeted information Oda needed, and it drove me back into all three earlier phases of my AREA research to get those critical data points."

John viewed the uncertainty from CAH as a reason to circle back to Absolute to study population data near the location for the roadside clinic. For partnering with the government, John's second round of Absolute work looked at national health data to see whether the feminine hygiene education campaign he'd run so successfully in Oda could be applied more broadly in other communities.

In his second round of Relative work, he verified demographic information and national health issues in Nepal. He looked for literature about the challenges and successes of expanding local preventative health campaigns in developing countries.

In his second round of Exploration work, John interviewed more lay leaders and local hospital personnel to better assess buy-in and budget projections for both options. He spoke with organizations that ran feminine hygiene education campaigns such as Purple Lily and 1000 Days. He had run a similar local campaign at his rural clinic and achieved a 70-percent increase in school attendance.

Claudia's CAH Exercise

When Claudia began her AREA research, coding looked like the easier path. There were fewer barriers to entry with many new schools opening, it was less expensive, and there were fewer prerequisites. But she didn't rush to judgment, and in viewing the information from other perspectives, the picture changed. Relative raised questions and even Exploration cast doubt on whether coding was a good fit for her.

In Claudia's CAH, she realized that there were some real unknowns about pursuing computer programming. Although the cost of the programs was lower than nursing school, the coding schools had a very low acceptance rate. In addition, she'd have to figure out before even starting which language she wanted to learn, so she'd need to specialize at the outset. It wasn't clear if the computer language skill she chose would retain its value, which might impact her ability to grow her career in the computer programming field.

Claudia's Competing Alternative Hypotheses		
	Nursing	Computer Programming
Cost	-	+ (less $$)
Time to acquire the necessary knowledge	- 18 months	+ 3-6 months
Likelihood of immediate acceptance	+	?
Specialization required at outset	+	-
Job skill set retains value	+	?
Room for growth within field	+	?
Job satisfaction/work environment	+	?

How could she know with confidence which language would be valued by employers in the future? How did she know if she'd be picking the language equivalent of a Blackberry versus an iPhone?

The CAH starkly displayed the concern that her new skills might be more quickly obsolete with computer programming. It also reassured her that nursing had a solid fundamental core. People need care when they are sick and, while the field could be interrupted by technology, the very basic skills would not completely replaceable by technology.

Moreover, Claudia recalled the conference attendees she'd met in her Exploration work and wondered how much job satisfaction she'd have if the environment she worked in didn't have some number of coworkers who were from her generation. Coding sounded exciting, but Claudia concluded—and it wasn't a complete surprise, as it had been building through her Absolute, Relative, and Exploration work—that she was more comfortable with nursing.

Pro/Con Analysis

This useful analysis tool dates back to a letter Benjamin Franklin wrote to his friend Joseph Priestly in 1772, who was wrestling with a thorny problem. The exercise asks you to combine your disparate pieces of research into two different coherent and cohesive narrative arguments to understand and analyze both sides of the issue. What might be the rationale for making a decision? What is the rationale for not making it?

Even though Claudia was strongly leaning toward nursing after her CAH exercise, she developed Pro/Con statements about deciding to go to computer programming school over nursing school. In her affirmative statement she wrote that she should pick nursing school over computer programming. In her negative statement she argued for the opposite outcome.

Cheetah Sheet 18: Pro/Con Analysis

1. Begin by writing out two brief memos: one framed in the affirmative saying what you should decide and the other statement making a case against the decision.

2. Next, write two separate narrative essays: one to support each thesis and list all of your reasons and evidence for each case. Be careful that both the Pro and Con cases are responsive to all major arguments addressing each point for both theses. If you make a specific case for your decision in the Pro case, respond to it in the Con case. This will help you to see where the argument might be flawed.

3. When you're done writing each compelling case, write up an analysis of your findings.

Here are John's statements for opening a second clinic and partnering with the government.

Opening a second clinic

Pro statement for a roadside facility: Oda may effectively increase its impact by opening a roadside healthcare clinic to directly care for more people.

Con statement for a roadside facility: Oda may be overwhelmed with traffic if it opens a roadside facility and its limited budget may constrain its ability to successfully care for the expanded patient flow.

Partnering with the government

Pro statement for a government network: Oda could successfully work within the government's network to expand its impact by conducting an education campaign.

Con statement for a government network: Oda could not successfully work within the government's network to expand its impact by conducting an education campaign.

The goal of the Pro/Con exercise is not to develop a view, but rather to step into the shoes of both views to develop a more complete understanding of the arguments in favor of and against your research target. The outcome should illuminate not only the "other side of the trade," but also provide a guide for further targeted research to investigate the answers to the questions that Pro/Con brings to light.

The following is John's Pro/Con analysis for opening a second clinic and for partnering with the government.

Pro statement for opening a second clinic: A permanent roadside facility would strategically capitalize on the strong grassroots and government support that the Oda Foundation has achieved to expand services to over 15,000 new patients. The Foundation's track record of success in the direct delivery of basic medical services, and the extremely low cost per patient, increases the likelihood of success. Additionally Oda identified a trained and trusted health professional who would be willing to work with Oda. Financially, this option would enable the organization to serve nearly 18,000 new patients for approximately $3.00 per visit. Given that the government is donating the building for the clinic, Oda should be able to secure the funds necessary to get it up and running and meet its operating costs. This initiative fills a clear and present need, and directly serves the Foundation's mission to reduce avoidable deaths in the Kalikot District.

Con statement for a roadside facility: While a permanent roadside facility would be a strategic move in leveraging local support and utilizing an existing facility, this project would still require extensive capital costs on the heels of a yearlong capital project at Oda Medical. Additional patient traffic has the potential to double annual operating costs, which for a fledgling organization will create significant financial challenges requiring over 100% increase in operating costs to over $90,000 a year, money which has not been identified. While this project meets a clear and present need, it could adversely impact Oda's reputation, as the organization is not currently prepared to raise the additional funds, to treat unanticipated illness, and to handle excess traffic.

Pro statement for a government network: Allowing Oda to use the government's network of 30 clinics would allow the organization to leverage a strong government relationship and existing infrastructure to quickly and cost effectively expand reach and impact. Population data indicates that Oda would expect to reach about 5,500 women and girls directly in an education campaign, increasing Oda's annual reach by 40%. Despite a lack of community trust for the current government health system, Oda's two years of proven success and a strong reputation in the district decreases any likelihood that the Oda name would be adversely impacted through this partnership. Evidence from Absolute, Relative, and Exploration show that there are a few national health issues that face all parts of the country such as nutrition and sanitation so that even though clinic needs may vary locally, there is reason to believe that Oda could develop one education campaign for the whole network. In addition, Oda successfully conducted a small-scale education initiative focused on early childhood development and girls' and women's health that reduced female absenteeism from school by 70%. There is promise that we can replicate this effort. Oda will be successful at keeping itself separate from the government's problematic reputation by building its own brand identity.

Con statement for a government network: While allowing Oda to use the government's existing infrastructure would enable us to reach a lot more people, we would also be relying on an unreliable and problematic system and would encounter potentially skeptical communities who are not familiar with the Oda Foundation's work. While Oda has conducted several successful small-scale education programs, it remains possible, albeit unlikely, that education initiatives will fall on deaf ears when moving into new communities.

The Pro/Con exercise forced John to flesh out and consider both sides of the government growth option equally. It evaluated his understanding of his Critical Concepts:

1. Did Oda have government and local community buy-in? It was still not completely clear that all local communities would buy in. There was no cell phone service in some of the areas and he'd have to visit these locales to know with any certainty.

2. Ability to execute? John believed that despite local variation in healthcare needs, Oda could develop a single education campaign to serve a national problem dealing with teenage girls and women's health.

3. Financial efficacy? John's realization that he did not have to cater to immediate local variability made him confident that there was good impact per dollar. He estimated that an education campaign could have a lot of leverage. The presentation could be built out once, tested, and then used in a widening circle of communities.

His concluding thesis statement from the Pro/Con exercise read:

The Pro/Con Exercise got me thinking about whether Oda could really handle a second clinic and successfully care for a larger patient population. For partnering with the government, it crystallized the importance of understanding local buy-in and our ability to be seen as distinct from the government's health system. This issue will determine whether or not we can succeed in working with the government.

To help him answer his new more targeted Critical Concepts, John used this next exercise, the Visual Map, to lay out the numbers associated with deciding whether or not he could continue to consider opening a second clinic or rule it out. Through the AREA Method, John's research was becoming more focused, guiding him toward understanding which decision he could make with confidence.

Visual Maps

Approximately three-fourths of our brain's sensory resources are dedicated to vision. That leaves only one-fourth for all the other senses combined. According to Dual Coding Theory, a memory theory that explains the impact of imagery on the brain, we process verbal and visual information with different parts of the brain. In other words, when we work only with words, we're not even using a quarter of our brain.

Because learning depends on both hemispheres of the brain—left hemisphere (verbal, logical, sequential, analysis) and right hemisphere (visual, emotional, intuitive, non-linear, big picture, synthesis)—one of the creative exercises that I ask my students to undertake is to put their visual thinking into play by using pictures to help them think about their Critical Concepts for their research target.

Translating visual thinking onto (virtual) paper is Visual Mapping. It combines words and images to create a visual record of your thoughts, literally revealing the "big picture." It helps you think about complex issues by demanding pictorial translation. For example, page 167 has a Visual Map I created for the AREA research of my World Bank Story that I created to show the AREA Method, using my World Bank Story as an example.

To see more Visual maps about the AREA Method and my World Bank story example, go to areamethod.com.

Research shows that 80 percent of people are visual thinkers, a statistic borne out by the vision-related metaphors that we use all the time, such as "Do you see what I mean?" or "I get the picture." Interestingly, many people are resistant to trying this exercise. When I introduce Visual Mapping in my classes, students often push back, thinking it's silly or reductive. But when they complete the exercise, they regularly comment that it forced them to get creative and that seeing a picture of their material helps them *see* their research question anew.

There is no one right way to make a Visual Map, but there are many benefits to it including fostering creativity, challenging your imagination, imagination, and sparking dialogue with others, so consider how you might visually display some of your research related to your decision.

Cheetah Sheet 19: Visual Mapping

1. How might you display your decision's "big picture" and/or details?

2. Can you connect your new information to existing knowledge in a chart, table, or graph?

3. Can you craft questions that you still need answered?

4. There are many websites and apps that can turn data into visual representations such as Piktochart, Sushi Status, and Sway, among others.

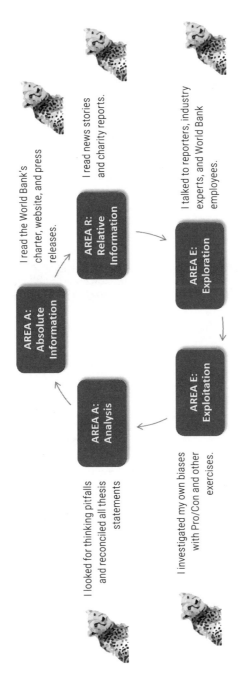

Is the World Bank an effective poverty-fighting organiazation?

I read the World Bank's charter, website, and press releases.

I read news stories and charity reports.

AREA A: Absolute Information

AREA R: Relative Information

AREA E: Exploration

I talked to reporters, industry experts, and World Bank employees.

AREA A: Analysis

AREA E: Exploitation

I looked for thinking pitfalls and reconciled all thesis statements

I investigated my own biases with Pro/Con and other exercises.

Put your map(s) in your AREA journal. Based on the information John initially gathered in his first round of research, he estimated that he could expect the clinic would serve 65 patients a day on
average. The two clinicians at Oda were able to see up to 70 patients
a day, so he was confident that he could staff the roadside clinic simi-
larly. He also anticipated that he'd be able to pay less for the staff at
the roadside facility than he paid his long-time clinicians who had
been at Oda and required a higher salary. The following image is
a Visual Map John constructed to compare the operating costs of
Oda's current clinic with the expected operating costs of a second
clinic. It's a simple visual representation of quantitative data in sche-
matic form, but it clearly shows the problem: the roadside facility
looked too expensive.

Oda Visual Map: Roadside Clinic Operating Cost Estimates		
Operating Costs	Oda Medical	Roadside Facility
Patients per day	40	65
Medical staff	2	2
Medicine costs per day	$87.00	$142.00
Cost of staff per month	$350.00	$300.00
Cost of staff per day	$15.22	$13.04
Average cost per day	$102.00	$155.00
Monthly budget	$2,356.00	$3,559.00
Yearly budget:	$28,267.00	$42,709.00

John also made a chart of expected capital costs involved in re-
pairing the building the government promised to Oda for the roadside clinic. The retrofit alone was estimated at $7,000 and then he'd
need to purchase diagnostic equipment for the clinic—another
$2,000. By visually organizing the information in two charts, John
immediately saw his problem: he would need to raise almost twice
Oda's current yearly budget, which was too much of a stretch.

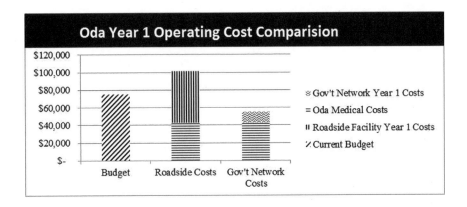

In hindsight, John could have considered his capital costs to retrofit a new clinic, just as he could have confirmed population data at an earlier point in the research process. But he didn't. Like John, we all have times when we skip a step. That's exactly why this Exploitation work asks you to revisit key pieces of information. And as you can see from John's map, it was really important that he did.

The realization about the stiff upfront costs led John to create a third chart comparing the upfront costs required for both projects. John recognized that the amount of up-front funding required to begin working within the government network was just 20 percent of project costs, or $2,020. This contrasted sharply with the roadside facility, which would require significant up-front funding, currently outside of Oda's budget. Additionally, this third map demonstrated Oda's ability to leverage a significant in-kind contribution for the government education campaign, which made up 43 percent of project costs.

Because John was leaning so strongly toward opening the second clinic, he went back to his Exploration work and interviewed staff at the hospital closest to the roadside clinic location he'd identified. He wanted to nail down what percentage of the hospital's patients were coming from the region around the planned roadside location and thus might come to a new clinic instead. He was hoping to see numbers that would make the new clinic option viable. Instead the Exploration work revealed that the hospital saw between 80 and 100 patients a day. If patient flow at the clinic even reached the low-end of the hospital's numbers, Oda would be overwhelmed.

His Visual Map thesis statement read as follows:

> The Visual Map shows that Oda would need to nearly double its budget to serve the projected number of patients who would visit the roadside clinic per day. It highlights our financial restraints in a way that clearly calls into question the viability of Oda pursuing a roadside clinic in the near future.

Scenario Analysis

Scenario Analysis is another decision-making exercise to consider possible outcomes and their implications after a given period of time. It is a risk-assessment technique that does not try to show one exact picture of the future, but instead consciously presents several alternative future developments or key factors that would affect a decision, such as the previous estimate for patient visits per year. It is not predictive, but meant to manage uncertainty. It is different from the Pro/Con exercise because though Pro/Con is about exploring both perspectives and making sure you understand them, Scenario Analysis is about understanding the magnitude of the outcome and the risks involved.

This exercise asks you to create several scenarios to show possible future outcomes, in particular a combination of an optimistic, a pessimistic, and a most-likely scenario. More scenarios are not necessarily better, as they can make the analysis unclear. The goal is to visualize and explore different ways forward.

A good Scenario Analysis shows not only a scope of possible future outcomes that are observable, but also the development paths leading to the outcomes. It does not need to rely upon historical data and does not expect past observations to be valid in the future, yet it tries to consider possible developments and turning points, which may be connected to the past.

Cheetah Sheet 20: Developing a Scenario Analysis

1. Upside: The first story might have everything proceeding normally with things falling into place and a happy ending, but should remain pragmatic and feasible. Tell the story in detail, laying it out step-by-step to reach the best possible outcome from your decision. Keep asking yourself, "What happened next?" Resist the temptation to skip to the end of the "story" without imagining the challenges or journey on the way. By describing the steps to a successful outcome for your research target you may generate even more scenarios for what might occur and when. If you can't figure out how they get from A to B, maybe B isn't as realistic as you thought.

2. Downside: Tell a different story about the same challenge. This time imagine the outcome of the decision going wrong, unexpected challenges impeding the progress, thwarting and derailing success. This scenario imagines the process being a struggle with a bad ending. Through this story, you may come to understand where the real challenges lie and how the decision might unravel.

3. Base: The final version is in the middle, neither great nor terrible. Perhaps it is a mediocre outcome, nothing disastrous yet no triumph. How does that scenario unfold? Again, fill in as much detail as possible.

4. Once you are done with the analysis, evaluate:
    a. Which of the three scenarios was easiest to imagine? Felt most real?
    b. How do historical data and insights inform the probabilities you attach to each scenario?
    c. What do you see now as most critical for the success of your decision?
    d. Where does danger lurk?
    e. To be successful, what needs to occur? What needs to be avoided?

To complete the Scenario Analysis, imagine the three versions of your research decision.

The Scenario Analysis will likely reveal new elements you need to consider that you may not have articulated, and questions you need to find answers for. It should reveal not only key choices that you may need to make in order for the decision to be successful, but also tease out important turning points that may make the difference between the outcomes. It shows you how your decision would be impacted by the various scenarios.

In the case of Oda, John developed estimates for base, upside, and downside cases to consider working with the government's health clinic network, as follows:

Upside

The government clinic network will provide a good way to address medical issues in a preventative rather than a curative way. In contrast to Oda's permanent facilities, an education outreach campaign would proactively get to the root of the problem, rather than providing palliative solutions. By educating women and girls, Oda's nutrition, sanitation, and child-care campaign may reduce female school absenteeism and improve health outcomes. We may also be able to collect other healthcare data that will prove valuable for Oda Foundation staff and the District Government in the future to improve healthcare treatment and outcome. This shift toward preventative care will reduce the long-term strain on Oda and government resources.

Downside

Grassroots buy-in will be challenging, as the Oda Foundation moves into new communities. Previous efforts were made successful by prolonged engagement and dialogue between the community and the foundation, a dialogue which doesn't exist in the new communities the organization hopes to serve. By partnering with the government, new communities will associate Oda with a weak and dysfunctional government, rather than a transparent development organization with good intentions. This could stymy education efforts, limiting long-term impact and adversely impacting Oda's reputation.

Base case

Working with the government's clinic network will be useful not only for the people of Nepal but also expand Oda's impact and data collection about health needs. Based on Oda's previous success, education campaigns targeted at early childhood nutrition and hygiene for adolescent girls will prove successful and require little follow-up. This initiative will be met with positivity and support, just as initial interactions with the people in Oda did. While mobile outreach will not replace direct delivery of care, these programs will be a valuable planning tool for Oda and create a resource for one of Kalikot's most at-risk and marginalized populations.

With all three possible outcomes laid out, John noticed that there were some real upsides and downsides to working with the government's clinics. Although he could not eradicate the risk of being associated with a weak government system, he could think creatively about how to mitigate that reputational risk. His thesis statement from the Scenario Analysis addressed this idea head on:

While there are substantive negatives to working with the government's clinic network, there are also some real positives in terms of expanding Oda's impact, improving basic health outcomes, and increasing our brand awareness in a low-cost, high-leverage education campaign that also allows Oda to collect data about health needs more broadly in Nepal. Given this conclusion, Oda may focus on developing ideas to reduce the risk of being associated with the government. For example, Oda may take several steps to protect its reputation, such as making sure to communicate that we are an are an independent organization when we give our seminars, and bring testimonials from prominent people in our current area of service to attest to the quality of our care and impact.

Conclusion

John's Exploitation work pushed his thinking about his decision. The exercises worked in concert to deepen his understanding of the challenges he faced. John's CAH revealed three assumptions that had to be investigated. If any were not true, they'd change his ability to successfully execute the strategy. Had he just done the CAH, it would have still been a game-changer. But by also completing a Visual Map and a Scenario Analysis, he pushed his thinking much further to problem-solve around the hurdles that his CAH revealed. He was, in effect, making his mistakes *before* he made them.

In the next and final AREA chapter, Analysis, you will bring all the perspectives you've researched into the conference room and let them sit around the table. In so doing, you'll reconcile the conflicts, consider all the key data and insights together, and assess your confidence so you can come to a conclusion regarding your high-stakes decision.

6

AREA = A: Analysis

To break a mental model is harder
than splitting the atom.

—Albert Einstein

In the Midrash, an ancient commentary on the Hebrew Bible, there is a story about young Moses being tested to determine his level of understanding. Moses' adopted father, the Pharaoh, loved him so much that he would kiss and hug Moses, who would then grab Pharaoh's crown and put it on his own head. This worried the Pharaoh's magicians. Would Moses eventually try to take Pharaoh's crown?

Jethro, one of the men of the Pharaoh's court, argued that Moses did not understand his actions and suggested that Moses be tested: Jethro placed a piece of gold and a hot coal before Moses. If Moses reached for the gold, he had understanding and should be killed; if he reached for the coal, he had no understanding and he should live. Moses grabbed the fiery red-hot piece of coal, burning his fingers and his tongue.

At this moment in your AREA research you are both Moses and the men of Pharaoh's court: You are trying to figure out if *you* have enough understanding. Are you reaching for a piece of gold, or might the outcome of your decision be a piece of coal that will burn you? You've gathered data from a variety of perspectives, you've evaluated your own understanding of the data, and now you are ready to interpret it all. Yes, you've been consistently pausing to analyze your findings through your many thesis statements, but through the process outlined in this final Analysis, you will determine whether your data yields gold or merely coal.

Before asking what it all means, the first step in analyzing your data is to decide if it is complete, if it is accurate, and if it can lead you to a decision. To do that, this chapter will explore solvability and fallibility: Might it be too hard to fully answer your Critical Concepts, and might your work have gone awry? Once you've determined what your data can and can't tell you, use the Analysis process to reconcile the many thesis statements that you've crafted throughout your AREA work so that you may make a thoughtful, well-researched, and confident decision.

Solvability

By now you've identified what puzzle pieces of your Critical Concepts are important and knowable, and which ones aren't. Are there any that may not be solvable by analysis or that may be too unpredictable? Although you might wonder why solvability is addressed here in the AREA Method as opposed to at the outset, it's because it's important to prevent upfront assumption and judgment about what is solvable and what data and information exists related to your decision. Although it is vexing to determine that there are "unsolvable" problems, many problems that appear unsolvable aren't.

Bill, for example, realized during his Exploration research that the problem he and his parents faced—of planning for every future contingency—wasn't solvable in the way he had hoped. When Bill, Lester, and Suzanne visited The Osborne and spoke with the marketing director there, they were dismayed at the high cost of the independent-living option and disappointed at the physical condition of the facility. What had looked shiny and new on the website was a bit worn and dated in person. Although the residents they spoke with had positive things to say about The Osborne, it wasn't the right time or the right fit for them. Suzanne and Lester were in far better health than the residents they saw. Suzanne remarked afterward that moving there would "make me age faster." Bill realized that although a continuing care facility looked like an answer to the unknowns that his parents would face as they aged, it wasn't the right solution for them. It was unclear what kind of care Bill's parents might need in the future and therefore they could not really determine if they were assessing the right qualities in the facilities they researched.

But Bill and his folks also realized that they didn't have to buy the Osborne package to get the services that the residents were getting. They had framed their decision as binary, when in reality the opportunity set was wider. They all agreed that Suzanne and Lester would look for a house where single-floor living would be possible, and instead of thinking about a second move, they began to explore the idea of a home with an extra room that might someday accommodate live-in help.

At the same time that Bill realized that he and his parents couldn't plan for every contingency, he also realized that he'd been thinking too narrowly about his decision so the problem wasn't solvable in the way he thought it was, but it also had solutions that he hadn't been able to see until he undertook his AREA research.

There is no systematic method of testing puzzles to determine whether they are solvable or not. Different people have different comfort zones and different skills when it comes to problem-solving. Whereas the exercises laid out in AREA Exploitation are meant to help you in taking a fresh look at your information, you will sometimes have to determine your own ability to judge the critical factors at hand, and you may have to either move forward without all the answers or reframe the problem.

For example, many students heading off to college don't know what they want to do or be when they finish college. They are going in without knowing their specific goal or its solvability. But not knowing what major you want to pursue or even what career you're aiming for doesn't mean you shouldn't go to college.

As he researched his expansion options for Oda, John initially felt that it was an unsolvable problem to determine how many patients might show up at a new clinic. However, when he created his Visual Map, he realized that he'd rushed through some of his earlier work. By taking the time to carefully go back and collect and analyze the data, John was able to make an educated estimate about patient flow. He did not need an exact number. The educated estimate told him the roadside clinic wasn't viable.

In general, if a decision is dependent on an unpredictable future event, you can sometimes use the past to determine a range of probabilities. The ultimate goal of thinking about solvability is to avoid spending a lot of time on things you're never going to figure out 100 percent.

For example, Claudia could assess the minimum amount of training that she needed for either computer programing or nursing, and she could calculate how long it would take and what the cost would be for that initial training. However, her research made it clear that she needed a kind of knowledge about programming at the outset that she didn't have. She didn't know exactly what kind of programming job would best suit her and that put up a barrier to entry because the training itself was specialized. Additionally, the coding world seemed to be one in flux. Yes, there was clear growth, but also a level of volatility and uncertainty that made Claudia uncomfortable.

For nursing, the training was the same for everyone and Claudia could more easily explore her options as a student without cutting off certain paths. In addition, as nursing changed going forward, her basic fundamental education would remain relevant and useful in a way that a specific computer programming language might not.

Still, some of the computer training courses prepared students far more quickly for jobs than the lengthy 18-month nursing programs. So in her final analysis, Claudia decided to take a free eight-hour online computer course offered by Girl Develop It. This confirmed in her mind that nursing better suited her; nursing was a more straightforward, stable career path. She placed programming in the "too uncertain" bucket and focused on nursing.

That being said, many things in life are a leap of faith and you have to decide if the risk is worth the reward. John's decision to open a first health clinic, even though he had no healthcare background, was a leap of faith. But for John, it was a leap of faith that has brought him not only success but a sense of worth and expanded opportunities to make a difference in people's lives. Just because you can't predict exactly how an action will turn out doesn't mean it isn't worth doing—and certainly doesn't mean you shouldn't do it.

Thinking About Mistakes

Beyond countering our adaptive ignorance and mental shortcuts, which is tackled in depth in the Exploitation chapter, where else might you face research flaws? Are you making a mistake in your analysis or might you be facing a failure of data? The power of discovering a mistake is not only that it gives you something concrete and detailed to fix, but it also allows you to advance your knowledge.

For example, skill at statistical analysis and skill at drawing findings from the data are often two different things. Statistics are often subject to error, and problems such as improper research sample size may obscure relevant results. To prevent such problems, consider the following points.

Cheetah Sheet 21: Getting the Data Right

1. **The Rule of Three:** Does your data come from *at least* three different sources? By collecting data from three unrelated sources, you can be more certain that your information is valid. Be aware of groupthink. When sourcing contacts, it isn't enough to have three sources if they are too closely related or depend upon the same data set. For example, at The Osborne, Bill arranged to speak with a nurse on staff as well as a couple of residents and a physical therapist. He didn't want to hear only from the marketing director, but wanted to know the inside experience of the place.

2. **Base Rates:** We all tend to ignore base rates, which are the underlying percentages or the actual likelihood of an event occurring. This tendency can lead to poor decision-making. For example, millions of people play the lottery every day in spite of overwhelming odds against winning the jackpot because media stories about winners—the exceptions to the odds—are more salient and memorable than the odds themselves. Despite having the lowest payout rate, the lottery is the most successful form of commercial gambling because we all rely too heavily on memorable events rather than base rates. We also all tend to overestimate our own ability to beat the odds.

    Micah's use of the AREA research process kept him from falling prey to this tendency. Unlike many other kids his age, Micah paid attention to base rates. That's why he went with the less prestigious college:

He knew the base rate was against him as a pre-med student, given that almost 80 percent of pre-med students don't finish the requirement. He wanted to try to get the best odds he could for completing a pre-med program.

3. **Data Fishing:** The findings from one data set don't automatically apply to another data set. Although it's useful to identify patterns and relationships between data, be careful to avoid data fishing, or taking more information from a data set than it actually contains. For example, weather patterns in Minnesota don't necessarily apply in Texas. For Claudia, national computer programming job placement rates were not as important as local ones. She knew she wasn't going to move, so she really only cared about what was happening in the New York City metropolitan area.

4. **Comparing Apples to Apples:** Review how the data is selected. Make sure you understand how a study was designed and conducted. For example, Micah was impressed with Johns Hopkins's ranking in *U.S. News & World Report* until he understood that it was based partly on alumni giving and professor salaries—data points that wouldn't impact his college experience.

In addition, mistakes can be made when numbers are reported in a vacuum. A four-year graduation rate of 85 percent isn't meaningful by itself. Is that high or low and why? Does it represent improvement or deterioration? Numbers need to be in context to be evaluated.

Pre-Mortems

One useful tool to assess potential pitfalls and mistakes is the pre-mortem. It's the hypothetical opposite of a postmortem, often used in medicine to allow health professionals and the family to learn what caused a patient's death. The joke is that with a postmortem, everyone benefits except, of course, the patient.

A pre-mortem, by contrast, is implemented before a decision rather than after it, so that the decision-making can be improved rather than autopsied. Unlike a typical critiquing session, in which project team members are asked what *might* go wrong, the pre-mortem operates on the assumption that the "patient" has died, and so asks what *did* go wrong. The task is to generate plausible reasons for your research target's failure.

According to researchers from the Wharton School, Cornell University, and the University of Colorado, prospective hindsight—imagining that an event has already occurred—is said to increase your ability to correctly identify reasons for future outcomes by as much as 30 percent. The exercise also sensitizes you to pick up early signs of trouble even after you've made your research decision. Micah, for example, knew going in that Pitt was not as well known for pre-med as Hopkins. So even before he arrived on campus, he knew he wanted to more closely explore how going to Pitt could "fail" to help him realize his medical aspirations. Then he could address these shortcomings ahead of time, and hopefully prevent them.

To conduct a Pre-Mortem, begin by imagining that your decision failed to turn out in the way you expected. Write down in your AREA journal all the reasons that you think it might have failed, including reasons that are less obvious, or seem to have a low probability.

John conducted a Pre-Mortem on joining with the government to replicate the health education campaign Oda had successfully administered locally that taught girls how to care for their period so that they didn't need to skip school during that time. He identified that if Oda didn't work with the communities and get their buy-in, Oda's efforts might fail.He also realized that if Oda was going to work effectively with the government, he needed to know that the schools maintained attendance data so that he could measure the impact of his education campaign; if he couldn't trust the data, and did not know where it might be weak or compromised, Oda's campaign might fail.

John chose to conduct a Pre-Mortem on both of these issues. He then developed a plan to prevent these failures from occurring. First, he decided Oda would partner with a few clinics to pilot both its education campaign and its data collection efforts. These initial clinics would serve as a "proving ground" for Oda.

Second, he decided that Oda would identify people in each community who could serve as emissaries for his organization. They could suggest to Oda who should be invited to education seminars, ensure those key people showed up, and introduce Oda to local school principals. This, in turn, would help John address his concern about poor data or poor understanding of flawed data. By getting to know the school principals, John could inquire about attendance records, record-keeping, and ensure better accuracy for his impact studies to find out whether attendance increased for girls who came to Oda's seminars.

In conducting your Pre-Mortem, one reason for failure may not be enough. Make sure to consider all of the issues that plague your Critical Concepts so that you may have an expansive view of potential pitfalls.

Cheetah Sheet 22: Pre-Mortem

1. What could cause the decision to fail?

2. What actions might you take if one or several of the events that could cause failure begin to play out?

3. At what point might you need to reevaluate the decision?

Once all possibilities have been written down, look for ways to strengthen your research in areas that demand it.

Write your answers in your AREA Journal so that you are less likely to fall prey to mission creep or to ignore bad news as it occurs.

Checklists

As the Nobel Prize–winning psychologist Daniel Kahneman writes in his book, *Thinking, Fast and Slow,* "Humans are incorrigibly inconsistent in making summary judgments of complex information." Checklists are an easy, low-tech way to guard against these kinds of poor decisions.

Although this book is filled with checklists in the form of Cheetah Sheets throughout, now is the time to ask yourself if you've really followed the AREA Method. Check your research. Have you done your Absolute research? Relative research? Exploration interviews? Have you checked your thinking?

But that's not the only useful kind of checklist. Another checklist to make at this point is your action plan checklist. As physician and author Atul Gawande writes in his book, *The Checklist Manifesto*, "Checklists seem to be able to defend anyone, even the experienced, against failure in many more tasks than we realized. They provide a kind of cognitive net. They catch mental flaws inherent in all of us— flaws of memory and attention and thoroughness."

Checklists have been used in aviation to reduce plane crashes; in construction to ensure that complicated building projects stay on schedule; in the treatment of heart attacks by EMTs and emergency room physicians, reducing the death rate from heart attacks by 38 percent in the last 10 years; and in myriad other fields. The World Health Organization has developed a Safe Surgery Checklist that is being instituted in hospitals around the world.

All of these checklists have one thing in common: they are de-signed to be repeatable and easily understood. Avoiding mistakes that you don't already know are mistakes will be really difficult, but avoiding mistakes that you *do* know are mistakes is doable through a checklist.

For John, his Pre-Mortem showed that if he could not get suf-ficient community buy-in, his education campaign could fail. He developed a thoughtful action plan to locate lay leaders to serve as emissaries for his organization. He also identified specific ways to connect with the personnel at the local clinics and with the school principals. His checklist was a simple to-do list that his team would complete at every clinic they visited; this allowed John to delegate the work but know that the important community connections would get made in a uniform way. The checklist would also serve as a record for the relationship with the local communities.

The checklist is a stopping point for two kinds of checks: one looking back and one looking forward.

Final Analysis: Reconciling Your Thesis Statements

Now that you've assessed the solvability of your Critical Concepts and the fallibility of your process and your data, you're ready for one more Cheetah Pause.

Your theses have provided you with clear signposts for completed sections of work and suggested your path forward for what to investigate next. They've also given you a way to document your process so that you can look back at your thinking as you move forward. Now is the time to pause once more, to bring them all together to serve as learning and teaching tools.

Thinking about the thesis statements this way—as learning and teaching tools—harkens back to the first chapter where I discussed process and content; content provides substance to the process, but is also derived from the process. A good process encourages good content. Your thesis statements together should represent the following components.

Cheetah Sheet 23: Appraising Your Thesis Statements Part 1

Do your theses have:

1. Findings: The facts of the case, the data, and the empirical results.

2. Interpretations: Explanations and inferences from the findings.

3. Judgments: Values and opinions about your findings and interpretations.

4. Recommendations: Suggested course of action.

To see them all together, write them down side by side in your AREA journal. When matched up, the many thesis statements should provide the scaffolding for understanding the complex issues you've investigated. Are the thesis statements consistent? Do they reconcile or diverge? Do they progress so that you are moving forward in your research toward making your high-stakes decision?

Cheetah Sheet 24: Appraising Your Thesis Statements Part 2

1. Do the thesis statements address your Critical Concepts?

2. How well do they represent what you've learned, understood, evaluated, and concluded about your Critical Concepts analysis? If they don't, revisit and rework your thesis statements until they are specific, factual, and actionable.

3. Are the thesis statements in agreement? If there is an unresolved conflict, it may be worth revisiting the issue.

4. Are the motives, considerations, and incentives of each source clear in the thesis statements and do you understand the bias inherent in the representation of each issue? If you don't, you may want to vet the information from that source.

Answering these questions further paves the way for you to objectively review the data you've collected, considering not only your information and analyses, but also accounting for the viewpoints of the sources you've reviewed. Altogether, do your statements suggest that you should circle back, do more work, and rethink your CCs, or are you ready to come to conviction and make your decision?

The following examples are summaries of John's findings from his many thesis statements that led him to expand Oda by working with the government's network of clinics. His complete thesis statements for all three of Oda's expansion options can be found in the appendix.

1. **AREA Absolute:** The government's fragile system needs assistance; demographic data suggests we could serve a lot of people, but that our impact might be limited by being episodic, meaning we'd be a "traveling doctor," visiting each clinic for only a few days at a time.

2. **AREA Relative:** The government system is weak and plagued by reputational problems that stem from absenteeism. We realized we did not want to too closely align with the government and it caused me to shift my thinking toward an education campaign instead of delivering direct care and/or training. I also learned that research showed that traveling doctors are not always effective in that they treat a patient for a moment in time, but then need to leave and so the care is not consistent. It made me consider my options and think about preventative care instead of palliative care. Specifically, I looked at education campaigns and found an article by the International Committee of the Red Cross, focusing on other basic healthcare organizations that have successfully implemented education campaigns in developing nations in South America and Africa. I found a lot of parallels and it gave me hope that maybe we could continue to research working with the government's network.

3. **AREA Exploration:** We confirmed that the government did want to work with Oda, but that the system was plagued with problems and that the District Health officer did not have a handle on what was happening on the ground at all 32 clinics. The research in Exploration validated and expanded upon what I learned in Relative, and I was able to identify other charities that were more mature than our organization that had conducted successful education campaigns. I interviewed a few of them and discussed evaluation metrics, then located medical supply charities that might donate supplies to us for a campaign focused on women and girls.

4. **AREA Exploitation:** The Competing Alternative Hypotheses Exercise really narrowed my Critical Concepts and sent me back into "A," "R," and "E"; then the Pro/Con exercise and the Scenario Analysis further shed light on how to understand the new data. The Visual Map made it plain that Oda was not equipped financially to operate a roadside facility and caused me to abandon pursuing that option.

5. **AREA Analysis:** The Pre-Mortem made me consider how Oda might fail working with the government in part by failing to get community buy-in or if we could not collect data that had integrity. That made me consider creative ways to address buy-in and settle on a plan of action to locate locally influential people who we could contact and explain our work to, and who then would act as emissaries for us in each clinic community. The lay leaders would help us recruit girls who would benefit from an education campaign about feminine hygiene and also introduce us to the local school principals who would in turn help Oda learn more about attendance data near each clinic to try to troubleshoot data problems before they might occur.

Together, these statements show a truncated path of findings for John's AREA research process, giving him not only the most important takeaways from each part of his investigation, but also his analysis, conclusions, and the implications for his next steps. His statements read like a story—a research story—and without reading the ending, it's clear that he's come to conviction. You know what will come next: his decision.

Here is John's final Cheetah Pause, his statement of work explaining his decision, and how and why it will be implemented and evaluated for success.

John's decision statement

In the next 8 to 12 months, Oda will accept the government's offer to use the government health network to disseminate a regional education campaign focused on feminine hygiene and nutrition for girls and women. The program is expected to reduce school absenteeism among post-puberty girls and reduce the instances of childhood stunting in the targeted population. Impact will be measured through follow-up surveys and data on changes in girls' school attendance rate and infant weight. Any problems associated with leveraging the government's healthcare network will be mitigated by laying groundwork in each community with a government clinic and by identifying local emissaries who can ensure local buy-in, successful implementation, and effective follow-through of our education campaign. The 5,500 individuals impacted through an education campaign will increase the number of individuals impacted by Oda annually by over 50%. Moreover, by seeing over 1,000 additional patients over the course of the campaign, it will enable Oda to continue increasing its direct service offering.

This thesis statement has all four of the recommended facets: It has John's findings, interpretations, judgments, and recommendation. It builds from his prior work, and he has defended it in thinking about where he might have made mistakes and in his Pre-Mortem.

For John, however, the final thesis statement, and the AREA work he did to develop it, had another unexpected but welcome effect: John was more clearly able to articulate his goals for Oda, as well as his process, and this led to greater donor buy-in. So by the time John completed his AREA research, *current and new donors had covered the full cost of the project.*

More broadly, by using data supported by AREA, the Oda Foundation raised more than $187,690 in cash and in-kind donations through the first eight months of 2015, more than doubling his 2014 fundraising total. In other words, by the time John made the decision to partner with the government he'd already fully funded the plan.

He'd identified new potential donors and was able to reach out to them as part of his Exploration work. "They were taken with our mission and with the depth of my focus, with my research and due-diligence," says John. "It enabled me to raise more money than I've ever raised before, and more quickly."

When John began his AREA research, he was almost certain he was going to open a second clinic, but he wanted some evidence to support his decision and he needed a way to fundraise. In his Exploitation work, John discovered that a second clinic was not financially feasible and might even bankrupt his charity. So he went back to Absolute, Relative, and Exploration research for partnering with the government. This led him back to his original plan and his core interest: keeping kids—girls in particular—in school.

For someone who wanted to start a charity to help kids stay in school, and detoured into providing healthcare, John's AREA Method research led him full circle. Thus the man who started Oda to improve school attendance found himself, unexpectedly, heading a larger and more impactful campaign to keep many more kids in school. By looking at the data, he saw a problem that many young American men might never have noticed or thought about. But he did. And then he went further: He solved this problem, giving girls the knowledge and hygiene supplies they needed to stay in school all month long, every month. He changed the trajectory of the girls'—and their community's—future.

Not every AREA research project will have such a "happy ending," but by following the AREA Method, I believe that you too will be able to better articulate your goals and your path to success. By making thoughtful, confident decisions anchored in research, you will be able to articulate the "what," the "why," and the "how" of your decision in ways that resonate with others. You will have written out the thinking behind your decision and your picture of success in a vivid, compelling way.

Conclusion

Blue Skies

Most of the mistakes in thinking are inadequacies of
perception rather than mistakes of logic.
—Edward de Bono

On the last day of 2013, my then-12-year-old son and I went to
New York City to see the Henri Magritte exhibit at the Museum of
Modern Art. The exhibit, titled "The Mystery of the Ordinary," was
organized around the concept that we are unable to really see what
is before us in part because we cannot easily escape our past experiences; they effectively "fill in" our present and taint our future.

Magritte consistently deals with the relationship between language, thought, and reality, and although his style is highly realistic, it is meant to undermine reality—what we think we know of
both ourselves internally and of our experience of the world. Thus
his paintings do what our mind inadvertently does: displace, transform, misname, and misrepresent images and information. Magritte
reminds us that we go about in half-waking states.

For example, in his painting *The Palace of Curtains*, Magritte
presents us with two frames containing the word *ciel* ("sky" in
French) and a pictorial representation of a blue "sky." Oddly enough,
both the word and image represent the "real thing." One works by
resemblance, the other by an intellectual but subjective association.
In other words, Magritte says, there are many ways to experience
"the real thing."

The fact that there are few absolutes—and many "real things"—is one of the reasons why I put together the AREA Method: to provide us all with a way to navigate our gray areas by managing for our cognitive shortcomings.

But even heightening our awareness of mental short cuts and inoculating our research against them is not enough to aid in making high-stakes decisions, and so the AREA Method does much more: It makes your work *work* for you, to make the process of collecting and analyzing data more effective, efficient, manageable, measured, relevant, reliable, and, most importantly, reusable.

Although research is about ideas, ideas aren't enough; there is an important gap between having ideas and making good decisions about what to do with them. For each of these individuals profiled in this book, the AREA process didn't help identify goals, but it helped achieve them.

It's easy to invest in ideas, but to make sound decisions you have to vet them, weed out the lemons, and have a way to develop conviction and maintain faith when it takes time to really see the impact of the decision.

History is littered with stories of good ideas botched by poor process. Take the story of PARC, the Palo Alto Research Center, the Xerox R&D laboratory that was the most successful corporate research lab in the 1970s. The engineers at PARC had brilliant, innovative ideas that were the foundation of many of the transformative technologies that we use today, including laser printing, the ethernet, the modern personal computer, and operating systems that fueled the rise of Microsoft and Apple. The problem: Xerox never commercialized these technologies; it was too slow to realize PARC's value.

Xerox hadn't determined its Critical Concepts, namely the purpose of PARC. Xerox didn't have a clear vision of what constituted a successful outcome for PARC and failed to see that it was an integral part of the company.

Xerox viewed PARC as being engaged in open-ended research, and it viewed itself as a copier company. The company's outlook was short-term while PARC's, by the very nature of pure research, was long-term. It was a classic case of misaligned incentives. And yet, that didn't need to be fatal if the company had had a clear focus on what to do about PARC's discoveries, namely to resolve that PARC could drive Xerox's success by providing it with innovative commercial products.

PARC's discoveries could have been "life-changing" for the company, but at the end of the day, Xerox lacked the right process to capitalize on PARC's brilliant and innovative ideas. As Steve Jobs said in a 1996 speech, "Xerox could have owned the entire computer industry...could have been the IBM of the Nineties...could have been the Microsoft of the Nineties." (*www.pbs.org/nerds/part3.html*)

PARC is a great example of a bad process. But a good process, if you follow it well, leads not only to logical thinking, creative insights, and an edge that gives you the confidence to act on your ideas, but also and importantly, it limits mistakes. John believed that if he had not followed the AREA Method, he would have gone ahead and opened a second roadside clinic and he might have bankrupted his organization within a year.

I believe the AREA Method is a process that enables you to take advantage of your ideas. With the right framework, the right approach to decision-making—*the right process*—you can turn good ideas into great thinking.

In teaching at both Columbia's Journalism School and Business School, and in my consulting practice, I have encountered different types of people with different backgrounds and different goals. In the Advanced Investment Research Class, I had students focused on being hedge fund analysts. In the Persuasion course, I encountered a diverse mix of all business school students. At the Journalism school, I taught students interested in all areas of journalism—some with no financial background at all. In my consulting practice, I've advised both not-for-profit organizations and for-profit companies. The common thread? A good research process improved all of their work—and mine.

That's the beauty of a good process. It allows you to see past your biases and your tendency to rush to judgment. It allows you to live your life mindfully, to increase your self-awareness, empathy, and understanding. It can give you the evidence and confidence to follow your heart, as Claudia did, or to see that the path that appeared easiest wasn't, as Bill did, or to do something unexpected, as Micah and John did.

John could have made what seemed like the right decision at the outset and bankrupted his charity. Instead, he followed a research process that showed him a path to a different and ultimately better decision. Micah looked past the buzz of a school to think about his goals and what he wanted to accomplish, and found that a different path would get him there in a better way.

The process also allows you to become the expert in your own life. Yes, Micah could have hired a college counselor who might have assisted him. Claudia could have worked with a life coach to make her career choice as well. Neither needed an "expert," because both became experts themselves, conducting their own research into an important personal decision.

At its heart, a good research process does not discriminate. It's an equitable tool that levels the playing field and can make each of us the real expert in our own lives. Even if you don't follow the full process, but selectively choose those research steps most relevant to your decision and your timeframe, AREA can be more than a process that you apply, it's a muscle that you build and it can become second nature; it can be part of the frame you bring to the world.

So at its core, although this book is about decision-making, about mastering and applying a straightforward process to conduct investigative research, it aspires to do in our work something logical and yet something, that at its heart, is very grand. Perhaps, as Magritte implies, it's impractical to try to master anything. But if there is anything that we *can* master, it's our choices. And so this book—and the AREA Method—strive to do something that many of us want to do with our lives: to make sense of our place in the world, to understand what we're capable of, and to move forward with conviction.

Summaries of AREA Processes and Critical Concepts

John

John Christopher is the founder of the Oda Foundation, a charity that provides basic healthcare to people in Oda, Nepal. He was thinking about expanding his charity when an earthquake struck Nepal. This gave Oda an opportunity to become a go-to organization for aid groups coming into Nepal to help people in this time of need.

What was the best way to transform his clinic into a more useful health service provider? How could he best serve the health needs of a country that looked different from where he'd operated for the past two years?

He laid out three different paths: Expand his rural clinic by opening a new clinic on a main road where his staff could service more patients; accept the Nepalese government's offer to partner with existing health clinics to expand the government's treatment and care; and invest in drones to drop and deliver medical kits.

Initially, John had one overarching Critical Concept: to maximize his organization's impact on the health of the Nepalese people by figuring out the best expansion path.

He began gathering Absolute data. This process clarified his CCs and by the end of the first stage of research, he had these Critical Concepts: He needed to understand whether each option had government and community support; he needed to know what costs were involved and what impact the option would have on healthcare in the Kalikot region; and he needed to figure out whether each option fit with Oda's core competencies.

As John conducted Relative and Exploration research, he ruled out drone delivery, as both the technology and infrastructure necessary weren't available in Nepal. John's research also helped him narrow down his CCs to three. First, did Oda have buy-in from both the government *and* the community for both options? Second, did Oda have the operational capacity to succeed in both options? Third, did each option make sense financially? Would he be using the charity's money in the best way possible?

Throughout his research process, John kept finding data suggesting that partnering with the government would be a mistake. Yet, by following the AREA Method, John fully understood the risks associated with opening a second clinic and working with the government.

Although opening a second clinic drew on Oda's core competencies, it was the option that had a strong likelihood of bankrupting the charity. Not only did it require hefty upfront capital costs to fix and retrofit the building, there was no good way to limit patient flow and ensure that it didn't exceed Oda's ability to cover the costs of treatment. Although this option met John's first Critical Concept, it did not meet his second, relating to quality care, or his third, related to financial efficacy. It was a no-go.

Recognizing the risks of opening a second clinic allowed John to focus on finding a way to work with the government, yet work around the government's poor healthcare reputation. By designing an education campaign, Oda could maintain its independence and identity and replicate a previously successful education campaign. This gave John confidence and certainty that his decision could succeed. He ultimately realized that partnering with the government met all of his Critical Concepts. It was his best option.

Micah

Micah, a high-school senior, was deciding between two very different college acceptance packages: Johns Hopkins University, with no financial aid, or the University of Pittsburgh, with a full scholarship. He only had a few weeks to make the decision. Micah knew he wanted to pursue medicine, and had already spent a summer working in a medical lab doing research. He was specifically interested in academic medicine and imagined pursuing a fellowship or additional research training after medical school and residency.

Initially, Micah saw his decision as figuring out which of these two college choices would get him into the "best" medical school. But as he began learning about the pre-med path, his Critical Concepts began to shift. Micah wanted to go to medical school, but discovered that the numbers were against him: at both Hopkins and Pitt, only about 20 percent of freshmen with a declared interest in the pre-med program actually applied to medical school.

Armed with this information, Micah understood that the critical question he needed to answer was not which undergraduate option would get him into the best medical school but which one would best set him up to succeed in completing the rigorous undergraduate pre-med requirements. He wanted the best chance to beat the odds and make it through the pre-med courses.

He realized that his problem was not solvable in the way he had hoped. With the vast majority of students dropping out of pre-med for a variety of reasons, Micah realized that he had to reframe his decision. By focusing on what he was solving for, he realized that his CCs were not really about which college to attend. Rather, a successful outcome for Micah meant recognizing which college would provide him with undergraduate research opportunities, a proactive pre-med support system from the administration, and the best learning experience that would competently guide him through the coursework so he could apply and get into medical school.

Bill

Bill wanted to help his aging parents transition from the multi-story home to a better living situation. He wasn't sure whether they should downsize in two stages—first into a home without stairs, and then into a nursing home or assisted care facility—or if he should find a housing facility that offered a continuum of care for the elderly.

Initially, Bill's primary Critical Concepts were that the facility offered a continuum of care and that it be located within 10 miles of where his parents lived. Many assisted living facilities offered a lot of bells and whistles—a busy and varied social calendar, trips into New York City, a variety of dining options—but Bill knew these features were less important to his parents than continuity of existing friendships and medical care.

As Bill explored some of the continuing care facilities in lower Westchester, he realized that 10 miles might sound close, but in Westchester, it was an enormous distance. In order to maintain both their social circle and their medical care relationships, Bill's parents could only look at facilities in a very narrow geographic area.

After a relatively quick website review, Bill refined his Critical Concepts to specifically address the idea that his parents would be able to retain their current medical care providers and maintain their independence in a place set up for an aging population.

During his Exploration research, Bill realized that the problem he and his parents faced—of planning for every future contingency— wasn't solvable in the way he'd hoped. Although he wanted one long-term solution, his parents did not really need to be in a segregated living situation in order to have their changing care needs met. When they visited a care facility in person, it wasn't the right solution for them. They all agreed that Bill's parents would look for a house in which single-floor living would be possible, with an extra room that could accommodate a live-in aide someday.

Claudia

Claudia had worked her way up from an entry-level position in advertising to a position in management throughout a 20-year career. But the advertising field was in flux, and Claudia felt that her expertise and experience were becoming unimportant. She watched as friends and colleagues were laid off, so she began to think about a career change. She had always been one of the go-to people at her agency when it came to anything computer-related, and had been reading about the boom in programming schools and jobs. Was there something out there for her? At the same time, as an undergraduate psychology major, she dreamed of working in the "helping" fields. She had read about the need for more nurses. Could that be a potential career path for her? Facing these two very different career paths, Claudia wasn't sure how to move forward.

Claudia's initial Critical Concepts were to have better job security and to be in a growth industry. Which of these two very different career paths should she follow?

When Claudia looked at the tuition numbers for nursing programs and coding schools, she had a bit of sticker shock. An accelerated RN degree could run her $40,000. Coding programs required a much smaller upfront investment, perhaps as little as $10,000. Still, she didn't want to choose a new career by upfront costs alone. So although she started with the numbers, Claudia didn't stop there.

By following the AREA Method, Claudia looked beyond the numbers. While coding schools seemed to have the lower barrier to entry, coding itself as a field had many barriers to entry. She'd have to "decide before deciding" which computer language she wanted to learn. Although today there was a dominant language, Claudia recognized that she didn't have the expertise to determine whether she was choosing the coding equivalent to the Blackberry or the iPhone. The schools and the field were still young, which meant a level of instability that she wasn't comfortable with.

Her CCs expanded from two to three when she realized during Exploration that the workplace environment needed to feel comfortable. As she researched her two options, she realized that the coding path was too foreign and volatile for her and the workplace environment skewed young and male. In order to better understand the coding world, and to make sure that she was not making the decision too quickly, Claudia invested 10 hours in an online introductory coding class, which she enjoyed. But she found the ceiling of her risk tolerance. Her coding future was too unclear, unknown, and unappealing.

For nursing, the training was the same for everyone and Claudia could easily explore her options as a student without cutting off certain paths. In addition, as nursing changed, her basic fundamental education would likely remain relevant and useful in a way that a specific computer programming language might not.

John's Complete Thesis Statements

The following are John's thesis statements and Exploitation conclusions for his original three expansion options. They are presented by option so you can follow the progression of John's research and thinking.

Roadside Clinic

Absolute

While a private roadside clinic would be a new healthcare delivery system, there is a clear and present need for such a facility. It would more than double our potential patient visits to over 20,000 annually, and would add three staff members and about $24,000 of expenses to our annual budget, necessitating an increase of about $36,000 in fundraising, of which approximately $20,000 would need to be identified.

Relative

Expanding Oda's primary care capacity to a roadside facility would complement our core competencies and serve as a significant lever while we explore potential growth; however, questions surrounding our ability to recruit and retain competent clinicians remain, as well as the size of the population that would use the facility. Relative data does not conflict with any previous financial assumptions, however, given the continued lack of data and potential downside financial risk, greater clarity is needed on both staffing availability and patient numbers as well as understanding whether the government will honor its promise to give Oda a building and what kind of capital improvements it might need.

Exploration

My interviews indicate that a second clinic is viable and realistic and would be welcome in the community, although the building being offered needs much more rehabilitation than previously expected. That would mean needing to raise more money than expected and would delay expanding our services by almost nine months. Exploration interviews also reveal that traffic at a roadside clinic may be much heavier than anticipated and there may be a more diverse and perhaps more serious set of illnesses than we've cared for in the past, raising concern about our ability to be effective both financially and operationally. Moreover, the government has expressed a clear preference that we work with their network of clinics instead of opening our own roadside facility.

Exploitation: Competing Alternative Hypothesis Thesis

Based upon the CAH exercise, the Foundation must further understand what patient traffic and health issues will look like in the new facility to understand costs and potential impact. Additionally, the cost of capital improvements to the new facility is a significant factor when weighing the two options and Oda's ability to execute.

Exploitation: Pro/Con Analysis

Pro Statement: Opening a second clinic

A permanent roadside facility would strategically capitalize on the strong grassroots and government support that the Oda Foundation has achieved to expand services to over 15,000 new patients. The Foundation's track record of success in the direct delivery of basic medical services, and the extremely low cost per patient, increases the likelihood of success. Additionally, Oda identified a trained and trusted health professional who would be willing to work with Oda. Financially, this option would enable the organization to serve nearly 18,000 new patients for approximately $3.00 per visit. Given that the government is donating the building for the clinic, Oda should be able to secure the funds necessary to get it up and running and meet its operating costs. This initiative fills a clear and present need, and directly serves the Foundation's mission to reduce avoidable deaths in the Kalikot District.

Con Statement: Roadside facility

While a permanent roadside facility would be a strategic move in leveraging local support and utilizing an existing facility, this project would still require extensive capital costs on the heels of a year-long capital project at Oda Medical. Additional patient traffic has the potential to double annual operating costs, which for a fledgling organization will create significant financial challenges requiring over 100% increase in operating costs to over $90,000 a year, money which has not been identified. While this project meets a clear and present need, it could adversely impact Oda's reputation, as the organization is not currently prepared to raise the additional funds, to treat unanticipated illness, and to handle excess traffic.

Pro/Con Conclusion

The Pro/Con Exercise got me thinking about whether Oda could really handle a second clinic and successfully care for a larger patient population.

Exploitation: Visual Map Thesis

The Visual Map shows that Oda would need to nearly double its budget to serve the projected number of patients who would visit the roadside clinic per day. It highlights our financial restraints in a way that clearly calls into question the viability of Oda pursuing a roadside clinic in the near future.

Exploitation: Final Thesis

The Competing Alternative Hypothesis Exercise really narrowed my Critical Concepts and sent me back into "A," "R," and "E," and then the Pro/Con exercise and the Scenario Analysis further shed light on how to understand the new data. The Visual Map made it plain that Oda was not equipped financially to operate a roadside facility and caused me to abandon pursuing that option.

Government Partnership

Absolute

Working with the government's health clinics would allow us to leverage a strong government relationship and existing health infrastructure to engage new communities, provide a wider dispersal of basic medical care and conduct a comprehensive district-wide needs analysis. The most recent census data validates this, indicating over 95,000 people and greater than 50% of the district live more than four hours from a road. This option would add one staff member and have a $29,000 budget of which about $19,000 would need to be identified.

Relative

The Relative research phase uncovered that the government's network is not reliable and that Oda might incur reputational harm by being too closely associated. To work with the government, we would need to have a more distinct and separate role. The research also revealed that education campaigns can be successful for basic health improvements. Perhaps this would enable Oda to work within the system while remaining independent. Oda could consider moving toward prevention rather than treatment, building upon Oda's successful prior campaign to keep girls in school during their period. Yet, the variety of clinics means that we need to explore whether one education campaign might be feasible, or whether Oda would be required to develop multiple campaigns, which might not be feasible given our resources.

Exploration

Partnering with the government is more problematic than initially understood in three ways: First it might entail Oda developing several different education campaigns instead of a single comprehensive program because the clinics seem to have different needs; second, it revealed that the government official in charge of the healthcare system does not have a clear picture of the day-to-day reality of all of the clinics; and third, it is unclear what expectation the government has for the education campaigns and this needs to be clarified. This again raises the issue of whether Oda might be able to work with the clinics to deliver a preventative care education campaign instead of treatment. If Oda can maintain its independence, this might be a solution.

Exploitation: Competing Alternative Hypothesis

For utilization of the government network, Oda must get evidence about grassroots community support and how much of a negative it might be to be associated with the government.

Exploitation: Pro/Con Analysis

Pro Statement: Government Network

Allowing Oda to use the government's network of 30 clinics allows the organization to leverage a strong government relationship and existing infrastructure to quickly and cost effectively expand reach and impact. Population data indicates that Oda would expand by about 5,500 women and girls directly in an education campaign, increasing Oda's annual reach by 40%. Despite a lack of community trust for the current government health system, Oda's two years of proven success and a strong reputation in the district decreases any likelihood that the Oda name would be adversely impacted through this partnership. Evidence from Absolute, Relative, and Exploration show that there are a few national health issues that face all parts of the country such as nutrition and sanitation so that even though clinic needs may vary locally, there is reason to believe that Oda could develop one education campaign for the whole network. In addition, Oda successfully conducted a small-scale education initiative focused on early childhood development and girls' and women's health that reduced female absenteeism from school by 70%. There is promise that we can replicate this effort. Oda will be successful at keeping itself separate from the government's problematic reputation by building its own brand identity.

Con Statement: Government Network

While allowing Oda to use the government's existing infrastructure would enable us to reach a lot more people, we would also be relying on an unreliable and problematic system and would encounter potentially skeptical communities who are not familiar with the Oda Foundation's work. While Oda has conducted several successful small-scale education programs, it remains possible, albeit unlikely, that education initiatives will fall on deaf ears when moving into new communities.

Pro/Con Conclusion

The Pro/Con Exercise for partnering with the government crystallized the importance of understanding local buy-in and our ability to be seen as distinct from the government's health system. This issue will determine whether or not we can succeed in working with the government.

Exploitation: Scenario Analysis

Upside

The government clinic network will provide a good way to address medical issues in a preventative rather than a curative way. In contrast to Oda's permanent facilities, an education outreach campaign would proactively get to the root of the problem, rather than providing palliative solutions. By educating women and girls, Oda's nutrition, sanitation and child-care campaign may reduce female school absenteeism and improve health outcomes. We may also be able to collect other health care data that will prove valuable for Oda Foundation staff and the District Government in the future to improve healthcare treatment and outcome. This shift towards preventative care will reduce the long-term strain on Oda and government resources.

Downside

Grassroots buy-in will be challenging, as the Oda Foundation moves into new communities. Previous efforts were made successful by prolonged engagement and dialogue between the community and the foundation, a dialogue which doesn't exist in the new communities the organization hopes to serve. By partnering with the government, new communities will associate Oda with a weak and dysfunctional government, rather than a transparent development organization with good intentions. This could stymy education efforts, limiting long-term impact and adversely impacting Oda's reputation.

Base case

Working with the government's clinic network will be useful not only for the people of Nepal but also will expand Oda's impact and data collection about health needs. Based on Oda's previous success, education campaigns targeted at early childhood nutrition and hygiene for adolescent girls will prove successful and require little follow up. This initiative will be met with positivity and support, just as initial interactions with the people in Oda did. While mobile outreach will not replace direct delivery of care, these programs will be a valuable planning tool for Oda and create a resource for one of Kalikot's most at risk and marginalized populations.

Conclusion

While there are substantive negatives to working with the government's clinic network, there are also some real positives in terms of expanding Oda's impact, improving basic health outcomes and increasing our brand awareness in a low-cost, high-leverage education campaign that also allows Oda to collect data about health needs more broadly in Nepal. Given this conclusion, Oda may focus on developing ideas to reduce the risk of being associated with the government. For example, Oda may take several steps to protect its reputation such as making sure to communicate that we are an independent organization when we give our seminars, and bring testimonials from prominent people in our current area of service to attest to the quality of our care and impact.

Analysis: Pre-Mortem

The Pre-Mortem made me consider how Oda might fail while working with the government in part by failing to get community buy-in or if we could not collect data that had integrity. That made me consider creative ways to address buy-in and settle on a plan of action to locate locally influential people who we could contact and explain our work to and who then would act as emissaries for us in each clinic community. The lay leaders would help us recruit girls who would benefit from an education campaign about feminine hygiene and also introduce us to the local principals who would in turn help Oda learn more about attendance data near each clinic to try to troubleshoot data problems before they might occur.

Analysis: Final Decision Statement

In the next 8 to 12 months, Oda will accept the government's offer to use the government health network to disseminate a regional education campaign focused on feminine hygiene and nutrition for girls and women. The program is expected to reduce school absenteeism among post-puberty girls and reduce the instances of childhood stunting in the targeted population. Impact will be measured through follow-up surveys and data on changes in girls' school attendance rate and infant weight. Any problems associated with leveraging the government's healthcare network will be mitigated by laying groundwork in each community with a government clinic and by identifying local emissaries who can ensure local buy in, successful implementation, and effective follow-through of our education campaign. The 5,500 individuals impacted through an education campaign will increase the number of individuals impacted by Oda annually by over 50%. Moreover by seeing over 1,000 additional patients over the course of the campaign, it will enable Oda to continue increasing its direct service offering.

Drone Medical Kit Delivery

Absolute

Drone technology has not played a significant role in the development sector in Nepal, but this technology is being explored in developing countries and has the potential for an array of medical applications. Given the distances and altitudes specified by Oda's pilot program, along with limited cultural and regulatory barriers, the technology has economic and operational feasibility. However, with more than 250 companies in approximately 60 countries producing drones, prices ranging from $500 to hundreds of thousands of dollars, funding and operating partnerships would be needed, as well as much more research to learn about the industry and logistics.

Relative

By engaging our existing facility, government relationships, and outside partners, we believe drones can effectively supply medicines, diagnostics, specimens, and vaccines to rural Nepal. We believe this concept has long term potential, however, a rapidly changing environment in the drone industry along with the unknowns associated with new technology, reaffirm the importance of finding a partner to offset financial and operational risks. Despite the long-term potential, the lack of reliable Internet in Nepal makes this option currently untenable. Additionally, drone technology has yet to be proven effective in addressing our primary mission, saving lives.

Exploration

Exploration research confirmed that drones require an available Internet connection at the base and receiving locations, which is not available in many areas of Nepal and is not currently viable.

Index

About the Author

Cheryl Strauss Einhorn, an award-winning investigative journalist, covers business, economic, and financial news for publications including *Barron's*, *The Council on Foreign Relations*, *Pro Publica*, *Foreign Policy*, and the *New York Times*. As the founder of CSE Consulting, a strategic consulting practice, she applies her AREA Method—initially developed to promote better decision-making in her journalism work—toward the success of businesses and individuals. A Columbia University adjunct professor, she teaches her AREA Method at Columbia Business School, having also taught it at the Graduate School of Journalism. To learn more about Einhorn, please visit areamethod.com.